# For The Record IX

Continuing Encouraging Words

for Ordinary Catholics

Rev. J. Ronald Knott

# FOR THE RECORD IX

## Continuing Encouraging Words

## for Ordinary Catholics

# *Also by J. Ronald Knott*

*An Encouraging Word: Renewed Hearts, Renewed Church*
The Crossroads Publishing Co., 1995 *(out of print)*

*One Heart at a Time: Renewing the Church in the New Millennium*
Sophronismos Press, 1999

*Sunday Nights: Encouraging Words for Young Adults*
Sophronismos Press, 2000

*Diocesan Priests in the Archdiocese of Louisville*
Archdiocese of Louisville Vocation Office, 2001

*Religious Communities in the Archdiocese of Louisville*
Archdiocese of Louisville Vocation Office, 2002

*For The Record: Encouraging Words for Ordinary Catholics,
Volumes I through VIII*
Sophronismos Press, 2003 through 2010

*Intentional Presbyterates: Claiming Our Common Sense of Purpose
as Diocesan Priests*
Sophronismos Press, 2003

*From Seminarian to Diocesan Priest: Managing a Successful Transition*
Sophronismos Press, 2004

*The Spiritual Leadership of a Parish Priest: On Being Good and Good At It*
Sophronismos Press, 2007

*Intentional Presbyterates: The Workbook*
Sophronismos Press, 2007

*A Bishop and His Priests Together: Resources for Building More
Intentional Presbyterates*
Sophronismos Press, 2011

---

Copies of Father Knott's books can be ordered via e-mail by
sending a request to: scholarshop@saintmeinrad.edu.

# For The Record IX

Continuing Encouraging Words
for Ordinary Catholics

## Rev. J. Ronald Knott

Sophronismos Press ◆ Louisville, Kentucky

FOR THE RECORD IX
*Continuing Encouraging Words for Ordinary Catholics*

Copyright © 2011 by J. Ronald Knott
All rights reserved.

No part of this book may be used or reproduced in any manner whatsoever without permission except in the case of brief quotations embodied in critical articles or reviews. For information address Sophronismos Press, 1271 Parkway Gardens Court #106, Louisville, Kentucky 40217.

First Printing: September 2011
ISBN 978-0-9800023-5-5

Cover Design © Morris Publishing

Printed in the United States of America by:

Morris Publishing®
3212 East Highway 30
Kearney, NE 68847
1-800-650-7888

*"To Lori Massey, who has offered constant support, encouragement and editing for the last nine years"*

# Acknowledgments

I would like to thank Mr. Joseph Duerr, former editor of *The Record*, our archdiocesan newspaper, who originally gave me the opportunity to write these weekly columns. I also thank Mr. Glenn Rutherford for giving me valuable advice along the way and Mrs. Marnie McAllister, who now edits these columns each week. I would like to offer a special thanks to Ms. Lori Massey for further editing and also formatting these columns into a book. Last of all, I would like to thank the many supportive readers who have encouraged me to keep on writing and who have taken the time to let me know how much these words of encouragement have meant to them.

# Looking for Goodness to Affirm

*I write these few words to encourage you.*
*I Peter 5:12*

"Time flies when you are having fun." It's hard for me to believe that, with this edition of *The Record*, I will have finished my ninth year of writing this weekly column. Four hundred and fifty columns in nine years! I had no idea, when I started, that it would come to this! When I started, I did not think about how long I would be writing. I was focused only on getting through the first few months without being "voted off the island."

Having a weekly deadline is like being chased by hounds that you can hear barking just over the ridge. Trying to stay ahead of the pack means that you can never let up. I have spent many a holiday and late nights turning out these columns. I am constantly on the prowl for ideas.

Writing is hard work. However, getting so much positive feedback makes it fun, and because it is fun, I cannot believe that nine years of my life have flown by so quickly!

It takes guts to stick one's neck out and reveal much about oneself week after week. While I have taken a few hits for some of my ideas and opinions, most of the feedback I have gotten has been extremely generous from a broad range of people from all parts of the diocese and beyond. Because of their generous feedback, I will attempt to make it to an even ten years at least!

Writing these columns has become an important part of my own spiritual discipline. It has been good for me to spend time reflecting on spiritual and religious themes in such a way that I can share it with others.

What I have learned from writing these columns, and in hearing the feedback they generate, is how many good and faithful people we have in this diocese. I am amazed at how deeply spiritual so many of my fellow Catholics are even today. I am amazed at their goodness. I am in awe of how much they have to handle in their lives and how well they handle it. I am humbled to know that I can offer them something they find helpful and useful in their lives.

My column, *An Encouraging Word*, deliberately tries to go against one of the strongest trends in our culture and Church. Today, political and religious beliefs are deeply felt and passionately argued. Mass communication, which often offers anonymity, gives people a cheap and easy way to demean the character of others. Increasingly, there is a tendency to disparage the name, reputation and motives of others. Reasoned discourse has been replaced by irresponsible demagoguery. Rude, crude and brash behaviors are normal. Civility is rare.

In this column, I deliberately try to look for goodness to affirm rather than evil to condemn. I try to offer people encouragement rather than condemnation. I try to celebrate virtue rather than "mouse" for vice.

*September 22, 2011*

*"I feel the need to encourage you to fight for the faith that we have handed down to the holy ones."*

—Jude 1:3

# Table of Contents

Preface: Looking for Goodness to Affirm .......................... v

A Salute to Those Who Provide Care ................................ 1
The Pitfalls of Multitasking ................................................ 3
"Go With the Flow" Can Lead to a Fall ............................. 5
We Need New Music for Our Old Song ............................ 7
When Will We Understand the Need to Change? ............. 9
Latest Book of Columns is Available ................................ 11
Respect for the Body in Life and Death ........................... 13
Principles in Examining Your Life .................................... 15
Encouraging and Helping Single Parents ......................... 17
Make Every Day a Day of Thanksgiving.......................... 19
The Damage of "Negative Talk" ....................................... 21
"The Things That Might Have Been" ............................... 23
Holidays Can Bring Sadness for Some ............................ 25
The Message of Christmas ................................................ 27
It's a New Year, with New Opportunities ........................ 29
Erasing the "Knots" in your Mind .................................... 31
Things Aren't Always as Bad as They Seem .................... 33
The Three St. Valentines Displayed Real Love ................ 35
Let's Embrace the New Roman Missal ............................ 37
The Spiritual Leadership of Married People .................... 39
Lent is Time to Refocus on "Walking His Paths" ............ 41
Lent is a Time to Change the Way we Think .................. 43
"Spiritual Seekers" Called to Lenten Missions ................. 45

# Table of Contents *(continued)*

We Can Choose How we Respond to Problems .............. 47
Resolutions Reveal Lack of Inner Strength ...................... 49
Catholics on the Margin Need Attention ......................... 51
Lent is a Time to Acknowledge Our Sins ......................... 53
The Spiritual Leadership of Priests ................................... 55
Gratitude for the Service of Missionaries ........................ 57
Are You Willing to Die for Your Faith? ............................ 59
Sharing Personal Stories Can Be Gratifying ..................... 61
The Church Needs Imagination and Ideas ...................... 63
Taking Responsibility For One's Faith ............................. 65
Advice to Graduates ........................................................ 67
Looking Toward Retirement ............................................ 69
Religion Should Bind People Together ............................ 71
A Salute to Siblings .......................................................... 73
Creating Yourself Takes Courage ..................................... 75
Live Simply to Live Well .................................................. 77
A Time To Laugh ............................................................. 79
Forgiveness Brings Freedom ............................................ 81
Choosing To Be Catholic ................................................. 83
Demographic of Priests is Changing ................................ 85
Children Have Religious Experiences .............................. 87
Three Phases of Spiritual Growth .................................... 89
"Why Are People Mean?" ................................................ 91
Self-Control Takes Practice .............................................. 93
Give and "Never Look Back" ........................................... 95

# A Salute to Those Who Provide Care

*Show compassion and kindness toward
one another. Zechariah 7:9*

I've written encouraging words to caregivers before, but the last time it was merely from what I observed. To need a caregiver personally, or have to rely on one yourself in a time of need, is another subject altogether.

Now that I am pretty well healed from my surgery, which was rougher than I expected, I want to salute my own caregivers — my sister Brenda and my brother-in-law Paul. They were with me in the hospital, stayed at my house the first night, took me to their home in Brandenburg for a few days, cooked, cleaned, did the laundry, brought my medicine to me, made phone calls, went shopping, changed my bed and bandages, and even cleaned up my vomit.

They have followed up with regular calls and promises to come at a moment's notice if I needed anything. I do not know what I would have done without them. All during that week, I kept recalling a line from an old comedy film, "Uncle Buck": "An imposition of this magnitude requires a relative."

What is so special about my caregivers is that they themselves have been through so much in their marriage, including months of caring for life-threatening major burns and painful skins grafts and, in the last few years, a long and painful battle to remission from bone cancer and endless follow-up visits.

In between, they successfully raised five children with all the caretaking that involves. The word "compassion" means "to suffer with." What made them so willing and able was due mostly to the fact that they know what it's like to suffer and to need help.

In thanking them, I want to offer an encouraging word to the hundreds of you who read this column who are taking care of elderly parents, sick spouses or chronically ill children. Sleepless nights, endless worry, sickening sights and smells, hours of waiting, exhaustion to the point of crying, cooking and cleaning, insurance papers, timing and keeping up with medications, lives on hold and bills piling up are only some of the nightmares many of you have been going through.

There's not a lot I can do for you but pray for you and let you know that I am aware of you. I have been sensitized to your heroic selflessness. You will be in my prayers on a more regular basis. When I go visit the sick from now on, I am going to try to make a better point of recognizing your presence and your compassion, your generosity and your service. Surely there is a very special place in heaven for those who find themselves in the demanding role of "caregiver."

When you are tired beyond tired, struggling against anger and feeling you are losing it, forgive yourself and give yourself some credit. No one can be perfect at it. Finally, pray that someday there will be a person like you to take care of you.

*September 23, 2010*

# The Pitfalls of Multitasking

*He who pays attention to his way safeguards his life. Proverbs 16:17*

"Multitasking" is one of those new ways of living that most of us are pressured to buy into to one degree or another. When you see someone in a car next to you eating a burrito, talking on a cell phone, smacking at a kid in the back seat and trying to drive at the same time, that person is "multitasking."

The problem is that when you try to pay attention to several things at once, your attention is never focused on anything well. It can be extremely dangerous to you, to other people's lives and to your relationships.

Because it makes you more prone to accidents, it probably doesn't save time in the long run, especially if you end up in the hospital, your children are starved for your attention, your marriage and relations wither up or, worse, you end up killing someone else.

It is not uncommon for me to see young kids walking down the sidewalk in front of my house holding hands. Quite often one will be chatting away on a cell phone to someone else. If I were his girlfriend and he did that to me, I'd kick him to the curb at the next corner. One hand says he is paying attention to me, and the other hand says he isn't.

I once heard a married couple "get into it" in a restaurant. It was their anniversary and they were out for a special dinner.

Obviously, the man was caught with a "roaming eye." Instead of focusing on his wife in front of him, who was totally focused on talking to him while holding his hands, he was constantly looking around at the "better options" in the room. She finally had enough and stormed out, calling him a few choice names as she did.

It is not uncommon to be talking to someone these days only to have them grab their cell phone, maybe even more than once, and say, "Let me get this," leaving you sitting there listening to drivel. My interest in any further conversation with the person at that point is seriously diminished, and it seems all I want to do is escape.

Multitasking parents often throw their kids in front of video games and the TV or ignore them as they scream for attention because they want to talk about what is going on in their lives at school or with their friends.

St. Therese of Lisieux, whose feast we celebrate tomorrow, has a lot to teach us "multitaskers." A nun at age 15 and dead at 24, she developed a spiritual practice called "the little way." She sought holiness of life simply by paying extraordinary attention to routine tasks and ordinary people. Her "little way" could not only lead us to holiness in the next life, but maybe a lot more sanity in this one.

Maybe the wiser choice is to do less and to do that better.

*September 30, 2010*

# "Go With the Flow" Can Lead to a Fall

*The intention in the human heart is like water far below the surface, but the man of intelligence draws it forth. Proverbs 20:5*

There is so much stupid advice floating around out there that people have bought into simply because it sounds easy and feels good. One of the poisonous tidbits is the expression "go with the flow."

It sounds like a nice way to spend a lazy Sunday afternoon or a summer vacation, but as a way of life I believe it is disastrous. I have met way too many victims of this brand of uncritical thinking. My advice is to do that for a day or two, but then get up and start paddling your boat.

"Go with the flow?" Are you kidding me? I grew up around people who taught a similar philosophy of life — that life is something that happens to you, and all you can do is make the most of it. That is a perfect path to victimhood, if there ever was one.

Maybe this is why we have so many adult children who don't have a clue what to do with their lives. "Going with the flow" has literally taken them over the falls, leaving them wrecked there. They are like the man on a runaway horse galloping wildly down the road when a farmer yells out to the frantic rider, "Where are you going?" The panicked rider, who had dropped the reins, yells back to the farmer, "Don't ask me; ask the horse!"

"Go with the flow?" No way! Sure, some people, through no fault of their own, have been dealt terrible misfortunes, but even many of them have thankfully refused to "go with the flow" and intentionally set out to rise above their limitations and excel, rather than accept them.

"Go with the flow?" No way! I am a believer in George Bernard Shaw's challenge: "This is the true joy in life, the being used for a purpose recognized by yourself as a mighty one; the being thoroughly worn out before you are thrown on the scrap heap." I believe in living intentionally, living with a definite purpose, with a determination to produce a desired result, living with a pit-bull kind of resolve to contribute something to the world and to become all that I can be.

When you become intentional about how you live your life, the entire universe conspires to help you reach your chosen goal, whatever it is. Jesus confirmed this when he said, "Believe that you will receive it and it shall be yours." (Mark 11:24)

"Go with the flow" may sound like a harmless bit of advice to soothe the troubled mind, but it can become an invitation to surrender personal responsibility for building a responsible and high-quality life. As William A. Foster put it, "Quality is never an accident; it is always the result of high intention, sincere effort, intelligent direction and skillful execution." Don't just "go with the flow." Get a life!

*October 7, 2010*

# We Need New Music for Our Old Song

*Behold, I make all things new! Revelation 21:5*

In times of stress and change — times such as these — people inevitably look back to some imagined "good old days" for a solution.

After the people of God left the slavery of Egypt and found themselves beset by trials on their way to the promised land, they grumbled against Moses and began to idealize the slavery they had left behind. Like an abused spouse returning to her abuser because the familiarity of her abuse is less scary than the fear of trying to making it on her own, they wanted to go "home." Some, of course, weren't even born in Egypt and had no personal memory of what was left behind.

It was Moses who had to keep reminding them, during the labor pains of change, to keep their eyes on the prize, to march on in the faith that God's promise of having their own land would finally appear before them — and it did.

St. Augustine preached powerfully about such nostalgia in the fifth century. "You hear people complaining about this present day and age because things were so much better in former times. I wonder what would happen if they could be taken back to the days of their ancestors — would we not still hear them complaining? You may think past ages were good, but it is only because you are not living in them." (Sermo Caillau-St. Yves 2, 92)

The great challenge of the spiritual life is to resist the belief that God used to be alive and active and to embrace the belief that the same God is alive and active now in the messiness of the world as it is. Did Jesus not say that "he is not God of the dead, but of the living;" not just a God of the past, but also of the present? We have a sacred history, a tradition, to hand on. But it is not the history that we worship, but rather the living God that came to us through history. Pope John Paul II was right about "the new evangelization." We need new music for our old song.

Instead of retreating to the imaginary safety of yesteryear and trying to recover some old form of the church from ages past, our job is to renew the ancient church in such a way that God can speak powerfully to people of today, in today's technological and highly educated culture. We cannot go back and pretend that our laity are not educated, deny that mass communication exists and hope that women will change their minds and give up their advancements. If we do, we will become irrelevant except to those who want a turned-in-on-itself, against-the-world, cultish Catholicism.

What's a believer to do these days? I like the advice of Bonhoeffer: "Faint not nor fear, but go out to the storm and the action, trusting in God whose commandment you faithfully follow; freedom, exultant, will welcome your spirit with joy."

*October 14, 2010*

# When Will We Understand the Need to Change?

*All that matters is that one is being created anew.*
*Galatians 6:15*

If you watch television or read the newspapers or surf the web, you may be coming to the conclusion that we are evolving into a nation of more and more individuals with no personal boundaries or self-control, desperate people fixated on an endless search for magic, external fixes.

We do it in politics. We are always looking for that magic political party or candidate who will "change things" without us ever having to go through any personal change. Alexis de Tocqueville had it right when he said, "A nation cannot be strong when everyone belonging to it is individually weak." Without becoming personally strong and more authentic individuals with internal strength, we are left to look for that magic political party or candidate to "make it all better for us" without ourselves ever having to change as persons.

As a country, when will we get it? A nation of drug addicts, petty and professional thieves, irresponsible parents, lazy crooks milking every system meant to help the poor and sick, unfaithful partners, bullying children, routine abortions, bulging prisons, a general lack of civility, a disrespect for public property, crooked lawyers, high school dropouts, people having babies who can't or won't parent, abandoned and neglected elderly, and unfaithful and incompetent spiritual leaders can never build a strong country, no matter who is elected to office.

The problem is that such people will only elect those who promise to give them their magic, external fixes and then crucify them in a few months if they don't. One party says "take care of yourself" while the other says "we'll take care of you." Both are failing. What is needed is inspiration, education and support for individual, internal change. We have to empower our citizens from the inside out.

As a church, when will we get it? Instead of preaching inner conversion and leading people through the process of personal transformation, we are fixated on our own versions of external fixes. We always fall back into trying to enforce external conformity through condemnations and canonical legislation when we realize that we are losing our ability to be real spiritual leaders. Religion will never be respected unless it can convincingly preach individual conversion and effectively lead people through personal transformation. Only then will they be able to choose the external conformity that society needs.

"All that matters is that one is being created anew." This is where religion is failing so miserably. We need to build our members from the inside out. Individuals must hunger and thirst for holiness, choose the path of righteousness and want to be transformed. Pastoral letters condemning what's wrong are ineffective. We need convincing voices that people want to follow, not more moral clarifications to which fewer and fewer people are paying attention.

Without internal personal conversion and personally embraced transformation, neither a strong church nor a strong country is possible, no matter who is pope or president.

*October 21, 2010*

# Latest Book of Columns is Available

*Write it on a tablet they can keep, inscribe it in a record. Isaiah 30:8*

When I left the Cathedral of the Assumption in 1997, I was approached by several people who wanted me to be their "spiritual director." Not having the time to meet the obligations of my new jobs and meet with that many people one-on-one, I tried to think of ways I could do "group spiritual direction" by making my homilies available to people who wanted them. I even thought about establishing my own website, but I never got around to it.

When the sexual abuse scandal was exposed in our local church a few years later, I became even more motivated. It occurred to me that I might try writing a weekly "encouraging word" in *The Record*. When Joseph Duerr invited me to send him a few columns, I did so with a mixture of excitement and terror. What if people did not like them? What if I could not turn out a column every week?

Bashful most of my early years, fear of rejection and fear of failure held me back from trying a lot of things, but in my mid-twenties, I made a conscious decision to start sticking my neck out more and start taking some calculated risks. Deciding to put myself out there in *The Record* every week was one of those decisions — maybe one of the best decisions I have ever made. As the famous Goethe said, "Whatever you can do, or dream you can, begin it. Boldness has genius, power and magic in it. Begin it now."

My columns appeal to "ordinary Catholics" more than the intellectual elite, and for that I do not apologize. As I read years ago, "If a teacher is not smart enough and in touch enough with the non-elite peoples to communicate his or her knowledge to them, then that person is in the wrong vocation."

You don't have to be a "writer" to be a writer. I encourage more of you to write for your own good. I have been journaling for most of my 40-year priesthood — not every day by any means, but regularly enough to track my own progress. I find it a good way to be your own "spiritual director" if necessary, especially if you are not fortunate enough to have found one available to you. I also find journaling a great way to pray with written words, to collect prayers and to collect my own insights and the spiritual insights of others.

When people started telling me that they collect my columns to read and re-read, I decided to put them in a convenient book each year for such reflections. I am happy to announce that Volume VIII is now available from the press. This latest volume, as well as Volumes I through VII, are available at Tonini's Church Supply, The Marian Center and the Maloney Center in Louisville, as well as The Scholarshop at St. Meinrad.

*October 28, 2010*

# Respect for the Body in Life and Death

*Some say there is no resurrection from the dead.*
*I Corinthians 15:12*

Two days ago we celebrated the Feast of All Souls, the day we especially pray for those who have died. It reminded me of a workshop that I attended for pastors of various denominations, sponsored by the Lilly Endowment, last January in Indianapolis. The purpose of the workshop was to discuss some of the alarming new customs that are filling the vacuum as Christian faith in an afterlife wanes in our culture.

With the author present, we discussed Thomas G. Long's book *Accompany Them With Singing: The Christian Funeral*. The author stated that because faith in an afterlife is less common, Christian funerals are being hijacked by staged, privatized productions called "memorial services" to help the grieving. They are less and less about the deceased.

Do we not hear people say that "funerals are for the living?" The dead, we are subtlety told, are only alive "in our memories." To answer the question in Peggy Lee's famous song, more and more funeral services tell us that this is all there is.

Most eye-opening was hearing that more and more Protestant churches do not even allow the body to be brought to the church. A Protestant professor of preaching at Emory University, Thomas Long, says that antipathy to the body now carries the day in many Christian funerals, particularly among suburban, educated, white Protestants, where frank acknowledgment of the pain of death and the firm hope in the resurrection of the body get nosed out by a sort of vague, body-denying, death-defying blather expressed in sappy poems that flat-out contradict our Christian theology of death and resurrection.

The sad part of it is that people participate in these services without even realizing this denial. To some Catholics' outright annoyance, our Church is trying to stand firm, even though the fight is on to keep some of these ideas from creeping into Catholic funerals. I have personally, more than once, wanted to scream when I hear the things that are sometimes said in those post-Communion "eulogies" that are gaining popularity at funeral Masses.

Christian attitudes toward the body were counter-cultural in antiquity, and it seems they are becoming counter-cultural again. Christians respect and reverence the human body in life and in death, and Christian funerals bear witness to the transition from this life to the next.

Let me end this column by quoting what the Catechism of the Catholic Church says about the bodies of the dead. "The bodies of the dead must be treated with respect and charity, in faith and hope of the Resurrection. The burial of the dead honors the children of God who are temples of the Holy Spirit. Autopsies can be morally permitted for legal inquests or scientific research. The free gift of organs after death is legitimate and can be meritorious. The Church permits cremation, provided that it does not demonstrate a denial of faith in the resurrection of the body." (No. 2300, No. 2301)

*November 4, 2010*

# Principles in Examining Your Life

*A voice shall sound in your ears; "This is the way; walk in it, when you would turn to the right or the left." Isaiah 30:24*

Have you ever taken the time to sit down and assess some of the principles you live by? Socrates said that "the unexamined life is not worth living."

I don't know if that is true in the absolute sense, but I do believe that people who do examine their lives, who think about where they have been, where they want to go and the paths they need to follow to take control of how they want to live their lives, are much happier people. Instead of living on "automatic pilot," following a "whatever happens, happens" pattern, there is a better way.

When you set aside time to examine your life, you have a much better probability of getting to choose your destination, to determine your path and to take control of what you want to be instead of being a victim — a victim of circumstances and a victim of other people's choices for you.

These are a few of the life principles that I have adopted and try hard to practice:

1. *God loves you, without condition, regardless of what you have done or failed to do.* Some grow up believing that God loved them when they were good, quit loving them when they were bad and started loving them again

when they shaped up. This last belief inevitably keeps God at a distance, but God becomes a trusted daily companion with the other belief.

2. *People may treat you badly, call you names, abuse you or try to block your growth.* Those things may hurt, but they only become problems if you start believing that you deserve to be treated that way. Treat yourself with the greatest respect, regardless of how you are treated.

3. *Do not let your fears rule your life.* The only way to overcome fear is to stand up to your own cowardice and face it down. Do hard things for your own good. You are more able than you think you are, and with God's grace, you are capable of things you have hardly imagined.

4. *Everybody craves love, driving them sometimes to look for it in all the wrong places.* Decide to be a love-giver no matter how needy you feel, and you will be showered eventually with all the love you need. Be proactive with your generosity, without any concern for thanks or appreciation, and your generosity will eventually come back to you a hundred-fold. Practice random and anonymous acts of kindness. You reap what you sow, be it good or evil.

5. *Keep no enemies and hold no grudges.* Make peace if you can, and if you can't, let it go before it eats a hole in your soul. "Holding onto anger is like grabbing a hot coal with the intent of throwing it at someone else; you are the one who gets burned."

*November 11, 2010*

# Encouraging and Helping Single Parents

*Show kindness and compassion toward each other. Zechariah 7:9*

This week I want to offer an encouraging word to those of you who are single parents heroically raising children mostly by yourselves.

According to a study released last November, there are approximately 13.7 million single parents in the United States today, and these parents are responsible for raising 21.8 million children (approximately 26 percent of children under 21 in the United States today).

Rather than getting a lot of support and encouragement, many of you are no doubt victims of other people's judgment that is the product of some pretty distorted information and stereotyping.

So what is the "average" single parent really like? According to the U.S. Census Bureau, (a) she is a mother, (b) she is divorced or separated, (c) she is employed, (d) she and her children do not live in poverty, (e) she does not receive public assistance, (f) she is 40 years old and older and (g) she is raising one child. An encouraging word certainly goes out to you. You deserve a big pat on the back.

Sure, there are many single mothers and fathers who do not fare this well. They are young, face unemployment or underemployment, have never married, live in poverty, need public assistance and have two or more children living with them. Contrary to popular opinion, they are not "average," but they, too, deserve an encouraging word and a large helping of compassion.

What can people like myself do, other than offer an encouraging word? Well, to begin with, we can at least shut our mouths and quit judging you without knowing what you are facing, what is being required of you, the difficulties you face and the things about which we have no knowledge.

I have a priest classmate in the Diocese of Joliet who went as far as adopting two children and successfully raising them. He now has "grandchildren." I am not that heroic, but I have been trying to help a single mother I know by paying part of the tuition for her to be able to send her three children to Catholic high schools here in Louisville. This doesn't make me a hero. I believe that it does "take a village to raise a child." I could not have made it through the seminary without a lot of help from people around this diocese I did not even know. It's my turn to pass on the blessing.

What can you do? First of all, take a good, hard look around and notice the single parents around you. Look for opportunities to offer them some encouragement. Volunteer to babysit, if appropriate, to give them a morning or evening to themselves or with their friends. Deliver a dinner, ready to go, when they are going through a bad time. Cut their grass once in a while. If you don't want to get "wrapped up" in their lives, think of something you can do anonymously. That, itself, might be more fun.

*November 18, 2010*

# Make Every Day a Day of Thanksgiving

*All powerful and ever-living God, we do well always and everywhere to give you thanks.*
*Mass Prefaces*

If I am not mistaken, Thanksgiving Day as a national holiday has gained in popularity since I was a child. It is now a "big deal" with many more families these days. That is, I believe, in the words of Martha Stewart, a "good thing!"

Sadly, though, Catholics have celebrated a "day of thanksgiving" every Sunday over that same period of time, but it, on the other hand, is losing in popularity. We call our weekly "day of thanksgiving" by its Greek name Eucharist, meaning thanksgiving. Just as our national holiday "brings our blood family together" in gratitude, our Eucharist brings our faith family together in gratitude.

Whether it is once a year or once a week, I don't believe that either is enough. I believe that our lives could be enriched deeply if gratitude would be practiced as a spiritual discipline every hour of every day — "always and everywhere," as the prefaces at Mass put it.

Henry Ward Beecher, an old favorite, put it this way: "Let the thankful heart sweep through the day and, as the magnet finds iron, so it will find in every hour, some heavenly blessings." This is the idea behind this whole column — running my spiritual metal detector over the world in front of me in search of someone to encourage and something for which to be thankful.

This idea of going through the day "panning for blessings" pays off. Ezra Taft Benson said it this way: "The more we express our gratitude to God for our blessings, the more he will bring to our minds other blessings. The more we are aware of to be grateful for, the happier we become."

Not only do we become more happy when we cultivate gratitude within our own hearts, it also makes us holy. William Law made this point. "Would you know who is the greatest saint in the world: it is not he who prays most or fasts most. It is not he who gives the most alms or is most eminent for temperance, chastity or justice; but it is he who is always thankful to God, who wills everything that God wills, who receives everything as an instance of God's goodness and has a heart always ready to praise God for it."

The ability to be grateful and express thanks is something that must be taught to us, and practiced, as children. When it isn't, we run the possibility of growing up believing that we are entitled to all that we have and more.

Sir John Templeton captured this insight better than I can when he wrote: "How wonderful it would be if we could help our children and grandchildren to learn thanksgiving at an early age. Thanksgiving opens doors. It changes a child's personality. A child is resentful, negative or thankful. Thankful children want to give, they radiate happiness, they draw people."

*November 25, 2010*

# The Damage of "Negative Talk"

*Encourage one another. II Corinthians 13:11*

With more poor schizophrenics left to roam the streets and more and more self-absorbed people with those "cell phone ear pieces" dangling from their lobes, it seems to me that I am hearing more and more people talking, louder and louder, to thin air.

While I'm at it, would someone please tell me what drives people to need to share their obnoxious car music with whole neighborhoods, their intimate phone conversations with everybody in the grocery store and every thought that crosses their minds in a text message? I will pay good money to the first company that comes up with a "portable jamming device" that I can carry around on my belt to protect myself from their total lack of civility.

I am not against one talking to oneself — in private. I must confess that I am always talking to myself, but hopefully I do it in my own mind or behind the closed doors of my home. If not, please, somebody get some help for me.

Self-talk can be both negative and positive. Growing up, I was not aware of what the therapeutic community knows today — how damaging negative comments from others can be to self-worth. Children tend to believe negative assessments of themselves from teachers and parents, developing a compromised self-concept when criticized on a regular basis.

It wasn't till I got older that I understood that I had joined them in criticizing myself. I can remember making the decision to stop my own self-defeating self-talk and start replacing it with positive and encouraging self-talk. It has been a long, hard road, because they say the ratio of positive-to-negative comments needs to be at least five to one for success in overcoming the damage.

Following the advice of Henry Ford, who said, "Those who think they can and those who think they can't are both right," I have been able to talk myself into doing things I never thought possible. I woke up every morning to a positive self-talk tape in my own voice for about five years. One of the many things on it that has come true is "I am a published spiritual writer." I now have fifteen books in print.

I still have a long way to go. I still say things to myself such as "I am not good at figuring out electronics," but if I stop, take my time and tell myself that "I can," I usually can. Negative self-talk increases my stress, and it stops me from searching for solutions.

I have fought negative talk throughout my priesthood — both in myself and others. In almost every assignment I have had, some priest has told me how impossible the situation was going to be. I found that the parishioners in almost every one of those assignments believed it themselves. My job, from the pulpit, was to get them to change the way they thought about themselves, and magic happened in every situation.

And so I say: "Yes, you really can!"

December 2, 2010

# "The Things That Might Have Been"

*Decide today whom you will serve. As for me and my household, we will serve the Lord.*
*Joshua 24:15*

It is hard to accept sometimes, but I believe we either choose to be the kind of men and women we end up becoming, or we become the kind of men and women we end up becoming because we fail to choose.

If we choose a life of commitment to doing the right thing, we become men and women of character. If we always choose the easy way and indulge our appetites without self-control or personal boundaries, our lives become burdened with an inward sense of shame, and we will ultimately forfeit self-respect as well as the respect of others.

If we try to split the difference, as many do, we end up in a purgatory of mediocrity and live lives of quiet (or sometimes not so quiet) desperation. Even a failure to choose is a choice that dooms some of us to a hell of regret, when we realize over and over again "the things that might have been."

Blaming others for who we are has been honed to a fine art these days. If we dislike who we are, we have been taught to blame our parents, our upbringing or our circumstances. Maybe we were powerless as children; maybe we were victims of circumstance earlier in life — but most of us are free to live differently in adulthood. George Bernard Shaw says,

"This is the true joy in life ... the being a force of nature instead of a feverish, selfish little clod of ailments and grievances, complaining that the world will not devote itself to making you happy."

It is hard to live intentionally in today's cultural context, but it is by no means impossible. The ability to say "no" gives us great power. We are free to decide the extent to which we will allow the culture to affect us. We have the power to choose what is good and reject what is bad.

Faced with an opportunity to choose a different way of living, many of us avoid making the choice. We are afraid of having to let go of some favorite old habit, afraid of what people might think of us, afraid of losing control, afraid of having to revise our maps of reality, afraid of all the work that real change will require.

As much as we like to complain, we often really don't want things in our lives to be all that different from the way they are. We both fear and crave becoming different from what we are now. When we choose the comfort of the familiar over the uncertainty of change, or worse, when we do not choose at all, we actually choose to commit personal and spiritual suicide.

The hardest truth of all just might be the knowledge that we have freely chosen to be what we have become, either by making good or bad choices or by failing to choose altogether.

*December 9, 2010*

# Holidays Can Bring Sadness for Some

*And Jesus wept. John 11:35*

For many people, Christmas is a wonderful time of shopping, dining, giving and just being together with loved ones, but for many others the holiday season can be a lonely, empty time — a time when loss, grief and loneliness come into sharp relief for those who have lost loved ones through premature birth, disease, violence, accidents or even natural causes at the end of a long life.

Today, I want to offer an encouraging word to those who are going through a rough time and feel their loss most acutely during the Christmas holidays — those who have lost children, spouses, parents or friends and still grieve deeply. When everyone else is celebrating and the air is filled with happy music, your pain can be exacerbated even more.

Sometimes this grief is new and raw, and sometimes it remains for years and stings without letting up. Some may say that such remembering is not healthy and that people ought not to dwell on such thoughts, but the opposite is true. Grief revisited is grief acknowledged, and grief confronted is grief resolved. "If you suppress grief too much, it can well redouble." (Moliere) "Grief is itself a medicine." (William Cowper)

Elisabeth Kübler-Ross, famous for her work in this area, has an important insight. "People in mourning have to come to grips with death before they can live again. Mourning can go on for years and years. It doesn't end after a year; that's a false fantasy. It usually ends when people realize that they can live again, that they can concentrate their energies on their lives as a whole, and not on their hurt, and guilt and pain."

Even when grief seems resolved, we can still feel a deep sense of loss at anniversaries and holidays — often when we least expect it. I know that I still get choked up during Mass on Mother's Day when we remember "those who have gone before us," though my mother has been dead for 35 years. Healing does not mean forgetting, and because we get on with life does not mean that we don't take part of the deceased with us. F. Alexander Magoun said this: "Tears have a wisdom of their own. They are the natural bleeding of an emotional wound, carrying the poison out of the system. Here lies the road to recovery."

Frank O'Connor said: "All I know from my experience is that the more loss we feel, the more grateful we should be for whatever it was we had to lose. It means that we had something worth grieving for. The ones I'm feeling sorry for are the ones that go through life without knowing what grief is."

Talking helps. It helps to have someone who will listen. A Turkish proverb says, "He that conceals his grief finds no remedy for it." A Czech Proverb says this: "Do not protect yourself from grief by a fence, but rather by your friends."

*December 16, 2010*

# The Message of Christmas

*I proclaim to you good news of great joy that will be for all the people. Luke 2:10*

The writer of Luke's Gospel has a fondness for the underdog. The rejected, the marginal, the left behind and the left out are more often than not presented as the heroes in the ministry of Jesus, for whom "there was no room in the inn."

The presence of shepherds, center stage, at the birth of the newborn Savior is so typical of Luke. Shepherds were marginally religious at best. They were despised and looked down upon by the religiously orthodox of the day. Yet it was to the likes of them that the "good news of great joy" first came.

Some of the best Christmases of my priesthood were during my years as pastor of the Cathedral of the Assumption. Because we were known for our welcoming of marginal, disaffected and alienated Catholics during those days, someone gave us the nickname "The Island of Misfit Toys."

Not knowing what that meant, I was told to rent a copy of the children's "Rudolph the Red-Nosed Reindeer" TV Christmas special to find out. In that animated story, the "Island of Misfit Toys" was that special place where broken toys could go to be repaired so that they, too, could be part of Christmas.

As far as I was concerned, that was one of the best compliments I ever received, especially in light of Luke's gospel. In my estimation, the church is supposed to be the place where broken people can go to be "repaired" through the hearing of "the good news of great joy" of God's universal and unconditional love for all people.

Luke's Gospel is the Gospel that tells us of the joyful recovery of the lost sheep, the enthusiastic welcome home of the prodigal son, the full day's pay of the late beginner, the "good" Samaritan, the Jesus who "welcomes sinners and eats with them," the sinful woman with the big heart who anointed the feet of Jesus, the story of the wedding feast where the poor, the crippled, the blind and the lame are invited.

Today I want to offer an encouraging word to those who feel marginalized and rejected by our church. "Do not be afraid; for behold I proclaim to you good news of great joy that will be for all the people." That "good news of great joy" is simply this: God loves you — always has and always will! You can reject it; you may never believe it, and others may try to get you to doubt it, but it is true, and this is what Christmas is about when all is said and done.

My friends, no matter how we are treated by others, no matter how low the opinions we have of ourselves, the message of Christmas is this — God loves us without condition, no ands, ifs or buts about it. Believe it, and act as if you believe it!

*December 23, 2010*

# It's a New Year, with New Opportunities

*I set before you life and death! Choose life!*
*Deuteronomy 30:19*

I stumbled onto a fascinating TV program several months back that showed what the earth would become without humans. It is based on a book, *The World Without Us,* by Alan Wiseman.

It showed how fast our massive, man-made infrastructure would collapse and finally vanish without our human attention. Just days after humans disappear, floods in New York's subways would start eroding the city's foundations and, as the world's cities crumble, asphalt jungles would gradually give way to real ones, and billions more birds would flourish.

Little by little, through erosion and decay, all our human handiwork would dissolve and return to a prehistoric wildness. Scientists call this process entropy, the spontaneous and unremitting tendency in the universe toward disorder unless there is an opposing force working against it.

Anyone who owns a home knows from first-hand experience that it will fall into ruin pretty quickly without regular maintenance and unrelenting upkeep. We all know a neighbor down the street who doesn't, won't or can't "get it." People go through the same process. We say that "they have let themselves go" when people neglect the care of their bodies. Good, strong marriages, neglected, usually end either in divorce, in a miserable existence or, minimally, in a quiet desperation.

Enthusiastic and faith-filled priests who do not do the hard things to "stay on top of their game" shortly become irritating caricatures of what a priest is supposed to be, hanging onto the trappings of religion long after faith has died in their hearts. We already know how disastrous it is for children when people have them without the ability or desire to "parent" them.

Bob Dylan used to sing, "If you're not busy being born, you are busy dying." Productive gardens need weeding; nice lawns need mowing; doctors need continuing education and we all need to maintain healthy life-styles and guard our callings against the relentless impulse to take things for granted. Even faith, unattended, is subject to withering.

Those of us who are married or live under other religious vows do not say "yes" to our calls once and for all. We must renew our commitments regularly, lest they be overtaken. We have to keep coming back to the task, knowing that the only thing scarier than showing up is not showing up. We need vigilance and stamina to keep "decay" at bay.

Annie Dillard describes this tendency toward "decay" very colorfully. "It is a lion you cage in your study, a lion growing in strength. You must visit it every day and reassert your mastery over it. If you skip a day, you are quite rightly afraid to open the door. You enter its room with bravura, holding a chair at the thing and shouting. 'Simba!'"

It's a new year! Will you do something to strengthen your faith, your marriage, your priesthood, your parenting, your health, your relationships in general — or will you just "let yourself go?"

*January 13, 2011*

# Erasing the "Knots" in your Mind

*With God all things are possible. Mark 10:27*

Father John Cole of the Archdiocese of Cardiff in Wales started it. After the retreat I gave the priests there last June, he told me that they had decided to call their follow-up program "Untying the Knott." A month later, I got the following prayer in my e-mail box. Actually, these plays on my name do not aggravate me one bit. I was actually honored by the priests of Cardiff, and there is much about this anonymous prayer that I like.

## The "Knots Prayer"

*Dear God, please untie the knots that are in my mind, my heart and my life. Remove the have nots, the can nots and the do nots that I have in my mind.*

*Erase the will nots, may nots, might nots that may find a home in my heart. Release me from the could nots, would nots and should nots that obstruct my life.*

*And most of all, dear God, I ask that you remove from my mind, my heart and my life all of the "am nots" that I have allowed to hold me back, especially the thought that I am not good enough.*

*Amen*

I resonate with the sentiments of this prayer, because they affirm some of my most basic beliefs about life, which can be summarized in a series of what have become some of my favorite quotes. "The biggest human temptation is to settle for too little." (Thomas Merton) "Impossible things just take a little longer." (Philo T. Farnsworth) "Start by doing what is necessary, then what is possible, and suddenly you are doing the impossible." (St. Francis of Assisi) "May you not forget the infinite possibilities that are born of faith." (Mother Teresa)

Why do so many people get bogged down in negative thinking and self-defeating talk? Because it was a normal part of my life as a young man, I have examined this very subject carefully. The answer I finally had to accept was — it is because we are lazy! When we declare a situation hopeless and impossible, we don't have to do anything — we're off the hook! Who would expect a thinking person to waste their time on something that is "hopeless" and "impossible?"

It doesn't take Oprah, Dr. Phil or Maury to realize that low self-esteem lies at the bottom of many of society's problems. These programs follow problems back to childhood, when important adults in their lives were either incapable or unwilling to "parent." Without their critical input, children begin to think that they are useless, life is hopeless and the future is dismal. When these thoughts become part of their way of thinking, many children grow up going down a path of self-destruction and violence toward others that is extremely hard to reverse.

Finally, if you are one of those who missed good parenting, your situation is not hopeless. Do what hundreds of others have done: "parent" yourself no matter how old you are!

*January 20, 2011*

# Things Aren't Always as Bad as They Seem

*Refuse no one the good on which he has a claim when it is in your power to do it for him.*
Proverbs 3:27

Many of you who read this column probably remember Charles Kuralt, a popular journalist who died in 1997. He did the positive and uplifting "On the Road" segment of the CBS Evening News.

One of my favorite quotes of his, one that summarizes his approach to the news, is this one: "It does no harm once in a while to acknowledge that the whole country isn't in flames, that there are people in the country besides politicians, entertainers and criminals."

Walter Lippmann, twice Pulitzer Prize-winning columnist who died in 1974, may have nailed it in a similar way when he said, "The news and the truth are not the same thing."

In the last seven years, I have met hundreds of fine bishops and thousands of good priests in my work as director of Saint Meinrad's Institute for Priests and Presbyterates. To paraphrase Charles Kuralt, "It does no harm once in a while to acknowledge that most priests are not child molesters, that most priests are happy and that there is again a growing number of healthy, young men who want to become priests."

You would never know that from reading the news. The same could be said about college students. "It does no harm once in a while to acknowledge that not all college students quit going to church, stop going to confession and never volunteer to do ministry in the Church."

Actually, 38% of college students attend church once they are away from home. At Bellarmine, where I am a campus minister, I pray with a full chapel almost every Sunday night, have heard a surprising number of confessions and know that many students volunteer regularly to do ministry there, in the larger community and even in other countries.

Similar things could be said about married people. "It does no harm once in a while to acknowledge that not all marriages end in divorce, that not all marriage partners are unfaithful and that not all young people are living together outside of marriage." Even though the news tends to focus on divorce, infidelity and cohabitation outside marriage, there are still many people who get married, live in fidelity and stay married throughout their lives.

We live in a world of downward spiraling talk that tells us compellingly how things are going from bad to worse. In reality, the more attention you shine on a particular subject, the more evidence of it will grow. Shine attention on obstacles and problems, and they multiply. Shine attention on possibilities and opportunities, and they multiply lavishly.

In our kind of world, people who articulate the possible are dismissed as dreamers persisting in a simplistic kind of optimism. The naysayers pride themselves on their supposed realism. They do not seem to know that what we say creates a reality; how we define things sets a framework for life to unfold.

*January 27, 2011*

# The Three St. Valentines Displayed Real Love

*No one has greater love than this, to lay down one's life for one's friends. John 15:13*

On February 14, many will celebrate the feast of St. Valentine, patron saint of love, young people and happy marriages. Even though Hallmark has tried their best to take him over, he still belongs to us.

Some Catholics have the notion that St. Valentine was "unsainted" in the 1960s when Pope Paul VI "cleaned up" the calendar of saints. Let me attempt to set the record straight.

While it is true that a review of the calendar of saints was done back then, St. Valentine was not thrown on the scrap heap. He was just removed from the General Roman Calendar, and the decision to celebrate his feast was left to local churches.

Not only was he not "done in," there are at least three different Saint Valentines, all of them martyrs, all of them mentioned in early martyrologies under the date of Feb. 14. One is described as a priest of Rome, another a bishop, and both of these seem to have been martyred in the second half of the third centuries and to have been buried on the Flaminian Way, but at different distances from the city. Of the third Saint Valentine, who suffered in Africa with a number of companions, nothing further is known.

The customs that we associate with Saint Valentine's Day undoubtedly have their origins in a conventional popular belief in England and France during the Middle Ages: that on February 14, birds began to pair.

For this reason, the day was looked upon as specially consecrated to lovers and as a proper occasion for writing love letters and sending lover's tokens. Those who chose each other under these circumstances seem to have called each other their "Valentines."

What can we take away from all this? One thing for sure — real love has more to do with the "laying down of one's life" of the three Valentine martyrs than the sentimentality of the Valentine industry. The priest, Valentine, was beaten with clubs and beheaded by the Emperor Claudius II around 270 for not renouncing his Christian faith. You don't see that kind of love artistically displayed on today's mushy Hallmark cards.

One of the most pervasive misconceptions about love in our culture is the belief that "falling in love" is love. There are two problems with that idea. The first is that the experience of falling in love is specifically a sex-linked, erotic experience. The second is that the experience of falling in love is invariably temporary.

Our second most common misconception about love is that dependency is love. Dependency is the inability to function adequately without the certainty that one is being cared for by another. People with this disorder are so busy seeking to be loved that they have no energy left to love. They only care that the other is there to satisfy them. Two "half-people" have never made a whole couple.

*February 10, 2011*

# Let's Embrace the New Roman Missal

*All that matters is the one is being created anew.*
*Galatians 6:15*

Like it or not, this is the year to implement the New Roman Missal. For a significant number of middle-aged and older priests and lay ministers, this presents a dilemma — especially for those who are stuck in their attachment to their own points of view and are not able to move from their individual points of view to a new communal viewing point. Having worked hard to implement change in a post-Vatican II Church, with its treasured experimentation and self-expression, many are highly suspicious that "they" are trying to take it all back.

Another source of their fear is a new generation of young Catholics who seem to them to be decidedly "conservative." While many of the previous generation grew up in a Church where personal opinions did not matter, these young Catholics have grown up in a Church where the opinion of every Tom, Dick and Jane seemed to have equal value. These new Catholics don't want to gather in a circle to hear what individuals feel about liturgy or brainstorm creative ideas; they want to know what the Church says is authentic Catholic liturgy. While the past generation sought experimentation in liturgy, this generation seeks orthodoxy.

I can understand their concerns. I witnessed many bizarre, but well-intentioned, homemade liturgical practices when I was the Vocation Director. I visited well over one hundred parishes. As a guest celebrant, I tried to go along, but several times I would leave shaken by what I had seen and witnessed and what I was asked to do.

Going forward, the ideal would be for the past generation to admit that some of the stuff done in the name of experimentation actually missed the mark, while getting the present generation to admit that some incredible work was done in bringing the laity into full and active participation.

Where do we go from here? Personally, now that it is a "given," I suggest that we embrace the New Roman Missal. I propose that we take what we learned during that post-Vatican II period of extended experimentation and move into a new mindset that I would describe as having a renewed emphasis on quality, not experimentation — from constantly rewriting liturgy to doing what's in the book (with its options) well. I suggest that we put our emphasis on becoming masters of the skillful use of the Church's approved texts in bringing our people into deeper discipleship. I suggest that we spend our time not on inventing more experimental liturgical practices, but on upping the quality of our liturgical practices.

All this offers us a blunt challenge. Let us focus on the skillful use of the Church's newest texts and make them come alive. Let us become masters in their use so as to be able to influence people to move from where they are to where God wants them to be — and that is to become better and better disciples of the Lord Jesus!

*February 17, 2011*

# The Spiritual Leadership of Married People

*Lord, you know that I take this wife of mine for a noble purpose. Call down your mercy on me and her, and allow us to live together to a happy old age. Tobit 8:7*

There are two sacraments directed toward the salvation of others — Holy Orders and Marriage. In other words, men are ordained and people are married in order to lead others to salvation. Most of us know that priests are spiritual leaders of the people they serve, but many do not know that married people are called to be spiritual leaders for their spouses and their children. Today I would like to say a few things about the spiritual leadership of married people. To do that, I will use the characteristics of a good spiritual leader identified by St. Bonaventure. St. Bonaventure, writing in the 13th century, identified six characteristics of good spiritual leadership.

1. *Zeal for Righteousness* — The first virtue needed in leading one's spouse and children to holiness is a zeal for righteousness, so that his heart is troubled whenever he finds anything unjust and evil in himself or in others. When he fails to address that evil, he bears the guilt of neglect of his duty as a spouse and parent.

2. *Brotherly Love* — The second virtue needed in the spiritual leadership of marriage is brotherly love or practical helpfulness for those in his care as regards both their physical and spiritual welfare. Just as they need protection from physical harm, so they need protection from spiritual harm.

3. *Patience* — The third virtue needed in leading one's spouse and children to holiness is patience. The responsibilities of marriage and parenting can be time-consuming and fatiguing. Often, appreciation is not expressed and direction is not taken. The work can be exhausting, the progress slow and the people demanding.

4. *Good Example* — The fourth virtue for the spiritual leadership of marriage is good example, being a model spouse for your partner and a model parent for your children. Actions speak louder than words. Spouses teach their children about the ideals of marriage most effectively through example. Partners teach their children about personal respect in the way they treat each other. Spouses teach their children about love of neighbor by how they relate to the communities in which they live.

5. *Good Judgment* — The fifth virtue needed in leading one's spouse and children to holiness is good judgment. Partners and parents must know the right thing to do and how to do it, and they must inspire those in their care to do it.

6. *Devotion to God* — The sixth virtue needed for the spiritual leadership of marriage is devotion to God, which gives them zeal for good deeds, strengthens their patience and clarifies their judgments. It is the foundation of all good example and the motive for the practical helpfulness of brotherly love. Practicing this virtue will lead to making both private and public prayer integral to their marriage and family.

*February 24, 2011*

# Lent is Time to Refocus on "Walking His Paths"

*Let us climb the Lord's mountain that he may instruct us in his ways so that we may walk in his paths. Isaiah 2:3*

Next week we begin the holy season of Lent — an annual retreat when we "climb the Lord's mountain" in order that God may "instruct us in his ways so that we may walk in his paths."

"Climbing the Lord's mountain" is a metaphor for simply trying to rise above the pace of ordinary living to refocus our attention and intensify our efforts on "walking his paths" more faithfully. To do that, we especially focus on the spiritual disciplines of prayer, fasting and almsgiving.

*Prayer* — Most of us tend to think of prayer as words we say to persuade God to do something he is not already doing. While it is true that we are invited to ask God for favors, the real essence of prayer is to ask God to change us so that we will want what he wants. After all, all God really wants is our good, anyway! Our Lenten prayer, then, is basically about our changing so that we will want what God wants rather than the other way around.

Going to daily Mass or saying the rosary is always good, but that does not work for everybody. If you have a hard time adding more prayer time to your schedule, try carving out that time by turning off the radio on your way to work. If you find it hard to concentrate, try praying for the people in the cars around you. Try getting up a half hour earlier than everybody else and sitting quietly with a cup of coffee. "Where there is a will, there is a way!"

*Fasting* — Often many of us eat not because we are hungry, but because we are trying to fill an emotional void in our lives. When we fast, when we cut back on eating, we are invited to feel the pain we want to avoid. Feeling it, we can identify it. Identifying it, we can address it rather than numb it with food.

It is a perversion of Lent to confuse fasting with dieting. Dieting is selfish. Fasting is other-centered. Be it your daily Starbucks or that second beer, monitor your feelings when you "deprive" yourself. Study your reactions and let them give you some important insights into yourself.

*Almsgiving* — When we hear the word "almsgiving," most of us immediately think of "giving something to charity." What we do in almsgiving is not as important as why we do it. Almsgiving can be selfish. It can make us feel righteous. What it is meant to do, really, is raise our awareness of our connectedness to others. It helps us remember that we are all in this together. "No man is an island." "We are our brother's keeper."

Ash Wednesday has a way of sneaking up on us. Let's use the next few days to get ready to go on retreat!

March 3, 2011

# Lent is a Time to Change the Way we Think

*"Repent!" Mark 1:15*

To discern the direction that his ministry should take, Jesus spent 40 days in the Judean desert alone with God. The "temptations" were merely possible options that he would eventually reject as not consistent with God's will for him. Unfortunately, we usually end the reading with "what he did not choose." It is the next few lines that give us the "answer" he came up with in his discernment.

Repent! (In Greek, *"Metanoiete!"*) Don't just seek to change things. Change the way you think. Change the way you look at things. Change the values you live by. Then you will be able to see that the kingdom of heaven is indeed at hand. What is needed, Jesus realized, is a new mind and a new heart that will lead to a totally renewed person. He realized that only a radical interior conversion of the person, not external cosmetic changes, would do.

In the nineteenth century, the British philosopher John Stuart Mill saw past the early materialistic promises of the Industrial Age when he said, "No great improvements in the lot of mankind are possible until a great change takes place in their mode of thought."

As more economies of the world teeter on collapse, as political situations continue to throw sparks that could erupt in an all-out explosion, as valuable resources are stressed and stretched and competed for, as marriages and families continue to unravel, as both political parties continue to let us down, is it not obvious to many of us that we are beginning to realize just how much we need a new way of thinking, a new way of seeing and a new set of values other than the ones we are presently living by?

Most people living in the United States today have sampled the fruits of at least a little affluence. We have been free of the desperate survival needs that haunted generations of human history and still haunt whole populations. Today we experience a different kind of hunger — a hunger for meaning. We seem to know, down deep, that we need to change.

Most of us are still locked into a view that the world can be saved through some kind of collective effort. "The government ought to do this or that." "The Church ought to do such and such." The fact of the matter is, as Alexis de Tocqueville observed, "A nation (Church) cannot be strong when everyone belonging to it is individually weak."

The truth is that the only thing that will save the world, and our Church for that matter, will be personal conversion on a massive scale. As individuals, we need a radical change in the way we think, the way we see and the values we live by. Only then do we have any hope of seeing our sacred institutions renewed.

Lent is a time to take a long, hard, loving look into our own hearts and ask God to make them new!

*March 10, 2011*

# "Spiritual Seekers" Called to Lenten Missions

*Be transformed by the renewal of your mind.*
*Romans 12:2*

Some of my fondest childhood memories revolve around attending Lenten "parish missions" every year or two. These preaching events were usually conducted by one of the Passionist, Franciscan or Dominican priests. It was the only opportunity to enjoy some extended preaching. They always seemed to be more exciting and challenging than the sermons we got at a typical Sunday Mass. In fact, some of them might be called "fiery" as far as Catholic preaching went. The whole idea was to get the congregation "fired up" about living their Catholic faith.

I've lost count, but I have conducted well over seventy "parish missions" since Father Bill Griner invited me to consider doing one back in 1989. The first one, which I repeated in several parishes in the Archdiocese of Louisville, the Diocese of Owensboro and the Diocese of Venice, Fla., was called "Reasons for Hope." I was even accompanied regularly by a wonderful group of liturgical musicians, led by Elaine Winebrenner.

The next one was called "Consciously Christian, Deliberately Catholic." I gave that as a follow-up in many of the same parishes, as well as several new ones. The third one was called "Change the Way You See." The fourth one was called "You Are My Beloved."

Because a set of parish mission talks take a great deal of time to develop and take up a weekend as well as three to four nights in a row, I had to give up doing them because of other commitments. However, I get seduced into squeezing one in once in a while, as is the case this coming Lent.

As part of their 165th anniversary celebration, as well as the dedication of their new church, I will be conducting a parish mission for St. Francis Xavier Parish in Mount Washington, Ky., this coming weekend at all the Masses — Saturday at 5 p.m. and Sunday at 7 a.m. and 9 a.m. — and All Saints in Taylorsville, Ky., on Sunday at 11:30 a.m. and Sunday, Monday and Tuesday from 7 p.m. to 8 p.m. This parish mission will be called "Renewed People for a New Church."

At the weekend Masses I will preach on the second reading and explore the question, "Do you know who you are?" On Sunday night I will explore the question, "Do you know God?" On Monday night I will explore the question, "Do you know how to become holy?" On Tuesday night I will explore the question, "Do you know how to be part of a family?"

Other parishes will be offering other versions of parish missions and extending an invitation for you to join them. The good people of St. Francis Xavier would like for you to know that you are welcome out there as well. Maybe one of these offerings will be something you might want to do as a "Lenten resolution." If so, pick one and fill your car with other spiritual seekers. You will be most welcome at any of them.

*March 17, 2011*

# We Can Choose How we Respond to Problems

*If you love those who love you what right do you have to claim any credit? Matthew 5:46*

One of the most useful insights I have ever stumbled across was one from the Nazi concentration camp survivor, Victor Frankl, in his book, *Man's Search for Meaning*. He wrote these deeply meaningful and truly useful words: "Everything can be taken away from a man but one thing — the ability to choose one's attitude in any given set of circumstances."

We cannot always control what happens to us or around us, but we can choose how we want to respond. Things do not always work out. People divorce. Employees need to be fired. Children break our hearts. Friends let us down. Parents fail at parenting. In a world where revenge, vindictiveness, reciprocation, retribution and retaliation seem to be the most typical responses, we can train ourselves to respond differently.

Today, I would like to talk about the virtue of magnanimity, meaning to be generous in forgiving, eschewing resentment or revenge, and being unselfish and other-focused. The word comes from two Latin words: magna, meaning great, and animus, meaning soul or mind. Being magnanimous means being "big minded" or "great souled." It has nothing to do with who is right or who is wrong. It simply means to freely choose to be "noble" regardless of who is right and who is wrong.

It is really about "making a good ending" by choosing to be "big minded" or "great souled" regardless. Magnanimity is possible only for those who are not addicted to being right and who do not have a burning need to be faultless.

In life, we come face to face with unexpected circumstances, people who let us down and things that do not turn out the way we want them to be. Misunderstandings, human mistakes, bitter disappointments and shattered dreams are actually part of normal living. The more important thing to remember in those circumstances is that what happens is often not nearly as important as how we choose to react to what happens.

It takes magnanimity to go through a divorce without bitter vindictiveness and revenge. This is especially true when children are involved. In such cases, we might not be able to teach them about the permanence of marriage, but we can teach them about how to be civil, gracious and respectful with adversaries. It is as much of a gift to oneself as it is to the other, because it takes too much energy to carry a grudge. It takes magnanimity to forgive an ungrateful or hurtful child and treat them well without being bitter, resentful, caustic and hostile. All the time and energy it takes to nurse wounds that we would as soon not heal is ultimately self-punishing anyway.

It takes magnanimity to forgive a friend and make the first move toward reconciliation without needing to exact an apology. That is noble indeed. Taking the high road of humility is not a bad road to take for a friendship worth saving.

*March 24, 2011*

# Resolutions Reveal Lack of Inner Strength

*I do not do what I want, but I do what I hate.*
*Romans 7:15*

By now, many of us have violated our Lenten resolutions more than once, and some have probably given up. That is exactly why we make Lenten resolutions — to unmask just how little inner strength we have, not to punish ourselves or to please a God who loves to see us suffer. The whole purpose of Lent is to reveal ourselves to ourselves. If we do not have the personal discipline to resist small things like a candy bar or a beer, how will we ever be able to manage the big things that we need to have power over?

Some people marry without much thought about whether they have the discipline to love the other, no matter what, until death. Some have children without the personal discipline necessary to parent effectively. Seminarians are put through years of intense scrutiny as to their abilities to remain faithful to priesthood.

There is a saying that goes, "Your anointing may take you places where your character cannot sustain you." In other words, it is one thing to pledge one's life to a high purpose, but it is another thing to be able to carry through on that pledge.

One of the most needed virtues today is inner strength. We live in a world of near total freedom, but we more and more lack the ability to handle that freedom — and because we cannot handle it, we run the risk of losing it.

This is a recipe for disaster, a disaster that is played out all day, every day, in the news. It used to be a problem pretty much identified with adolescence. Never having had to develop inner strength growing up, more and more adults today go into their middle years stuck in adolescence.

Inner strength consists of willpower, self-discipline, detachment, persistence and the ability to concentrate — the most important of which may be willpower and self-discipline.

Willpower is the inner strength necessary to make decisions, to take action and to handle any aim or task, regardless of inner and outer resistance, discomfort or difficulties. Willpower is manifested in the ability to overcome laziness, temptations and negative habits and to carry out actions, even if they require effort, are unpleasant and tedious, or run contrary to normal behavior.

Self-discipline is the ability to reject instant gratification or pleasure in favor of something better or a higher goal. Self-discipline manifests itself in the ability to stick to actions or plans in spite of obstacles, difficulties or unpleasantness until they are realized.

Inner strength can be developed through focused practice, but only after we become clear about what we want and know what we must do in order to have what we seek. Inner strength gives us the ability to do hard things for our own good. Lenten resolutions reveal to us how much, or how little, inner strength we actually have.

*March 31, 2011*

# Catholics on the Margin Need Attention

*Who among you would not leave the ninety-nine and go after the lost one? Luke 15:4*

Not a week goes by that I don't hear from another Catholic hanging on by their fingernails. Throughout my priesthood, I have always seemed to attract them, and this column has been my way, these last eight years, of offering them an encouraging word.

The writer of Luke's gospel presents Jesus as having a special fondness for the underdog, the rejected, the marginal, the left behind, the left out and those hanging on by their fingernails. They are, more often than not, presented as the heroes in the stories of Jesus. Maybe that's why I have always had a special love for the Gospel of Luke — for most of my life I have identified with the likes of the lost sheep, the prodigal son, the worker who arrived late in the day, and those rounded up from the highways and byways and invited in to the party.

The Church is made up of some wonderfully faithful Catholics. They rarely miss Mass; they go to parish functions, take advantage of faith formation opportunities, support the parish financially, participate in its social service ministries, value strong family life and seek out opportunities to socialize with other Catholics. They are the ones who lift the heavy end of keeping the Church going, and for that they get the lion's share of the Church's attention.

There is, however, a group almost as big — and growing — that the Church is called to minister to as well. Some call them the "second largest denomination" in the United States. They may still be registered in a parish but attend Mass infrequently, only on holidays or not at all. They do not participate in parish activities, even though some of them send their children to sacramental preparation or religious education. They are not regular contributors. They may identify themselves as "Catholics," having been "raised Catholic" or even "former Catholics."

They are not all alike. Some are mad; some are sad; some are merely culturally different, and many of them are just flat-out bored with all the Church has to offer.

The "mad" are those who harbor various degrees of anger and resentment because of having been hurt, abused or neglected by clergy, religious or other church workers. The "sad" are those who feel separated from the Church because of marriage, divorce, sexual orientation or some doctrinal issue. Typically, many of these feel a sense of loss and still crave being included.

The culturally different feel they do not fit in or may not find people like themselves. The biggest group of all are probably those who have no particular complaint but have grown steadily weaker in the practice of the faith because they are bored with what the Church offers or how it offers it. Many young adults find themselves here.

It is to those on the edges of the flock that a good shepherd needs to pay special attention.

*April 7, 2011*

# Lent is a Time to Acknowledge Our Sins

*"The woman whom you put here with me — she gave me the fruit from the tree, and so I ate it." "The serpent tricked me into it, so I ate it."*
*Genesis 3:13*

- "It wasn't my fault!"
- "If my parents hadn't been so defective, I would not have turned to crime!"
- "I couldn't help it. I was drunk!"
- "I'm only human!"
- "I didn't do anything that everyone else isn't doing!"
- "I don't know! It just happened!"

From the very beginning, man has tended to project farther and farther from himself his responsibility for the evil that he does and the evil that goes on around him. In the story of creation, Adam blames Eve and Eve blames the serpent for the first sin. The first Letter of John cuts through our denials when it says, "If we say we are without sin, we deceive ourselves, and the truth is not in us."

Comedian Flip Wilson has gone the way of all old comedians, but his character "Geraldine" lives on in the many guests of TV shows like Jerry Springer. "Geraldine" used to squeal, "The Devil made me do it!" If you listen to the stream of pathetic guests and hear about their outrageous behaviors, you will realize right away that they have one thing in common — somebody or something else is always responsible.

If they are caught sleeping with their daughter's boyfriend, it was because they were drunk. If they are caught in adultery, it was because their spouse wasn't giving them the attention they deserved. If they are discovered committing incest with their sister, it was because "she came on to me."

Besides denying personal responsibility for the evil that we do, or that goes on around us, we project responsibility farther and farther from us by giving our sins new names. Adultery is often referred to "having an affair" or "playing around." Stealing is downgraded to "taking a few things from work" or "creative bookkeeping."

Even our government has done it. When the Nixon administration was confronted with "breaking and entering," the White House dismissed it as "misguided zeal." Murder and assassinations in Central America were once renamed by our State Department as "unlawful deprivation of life."

Sometimes we even elevate sin to the status of a virtue. Killing the terminally ill is often promoted under the nice-sounding banner of "mercy" killing or "euthanasia" (a Greek word meaning "good death").

We are closing yet another Lenten season — a time to face the truth about ourselves, a time to own and name our sins. Lent challenges us to admit the lies we try to tell ourselves and the lies others try to get us to believe.

Because the truth often hurts, we tend to turn away from it, deny it, numb it or cover it up. Avoidance settles for chronic, dull pain rather than brief, acute confrontation. It is in facing the truth, however painful, that we are ultimately set free.

*April 14, 2011*

# The Spiritual Leadership of Priests

*They have sown much, but brought in little; have eaten plenty, but have not been satisfied; have drunk much, but have not been exhilarated; clothed themselves well, but have not been warmed; earned wages for a bag with holes in it.*
Haggai 1:6

On this Holy Thursday, when we celebrate the institution of the priesthood, I would like to say a few words about the spiritual leadership of priests.

One of the most serious problems facing Catholicism today is the quality of its spiritual leadership in the face of deteriorating communal values and religious practice. It is no longer good enough for us priests to simply be priests; we have to be able to priest! By that I mean we can never be satisfied with simply being designated spiritual leaders; we must strive, with God's grace, to become real spiritual leaders.

I define "spiritual leadership" as the ability to influence people — through invitation, persuasion, example and the skillful use of the Church's rituals — to move from where they are to where God wants them to be.

We surely know today that organized religion has lost its power to impose unquestioned rules on the behavior of its members. This turn of events frustrates many priests, leaving them with a propensity to blame the laity for their lack of faith and the culture for its "secularism" and "moral relativism" in increasingly shrill denouncements.

No amount of ranting and raving, however, about how we ought to be listened to will fix this. The fact of the matter is that in a society where "a consumer" is a primary self-definition, we religious leaders have to not only know what the truth is and believe it ourselves, we also have to be able to sell that truth to others. We have to be able to convince people to see it, accept it and live it. We need to be more than right. We need to be convincing as well.

The more we priests lack the ability to influence people, the more we tend to blame, criticize and condemn. Silly and counter-productive rants about "secularism" and "moral relativism" merely expose our lack of spiritual leadership abilities. The truth is, there is an amazing lack of dynamism in the Church's designated leaders and in its pastoral structures for evangelization in a changing cultural climate. And that culture seems to be telling us that it is time to "shut up or put up."

What is needed are priests who are capable of telling people about the love of God in language that no longer sounds hackneyed and archaic, but in convincing language that resonates with authority and conviction. It is not good enough for us to believe that "grass is good" and "water is necessary"; we have to be able to find it and to lead our people to it — sometimes in a barren spiritual landscape. Our people need what John Paul II called "incarnations of the Good Shepherd's love."

*April 21, 2011*

# Gratitude for the Service of Missionaries

*Go out and make disciples of all nations, teaching them to observe all that I have commanded you.*
*Matthew 29: 19,20*

In my work at Saint Meinrad Seminary, I am constantly reminded of a prediction I remember hearing when I was a student there in the 1960s. I remember clipping an article out of a Catholic weekly and saving it. I probably still have it tucked away in some book somewhere. It said that we would soon see the day when the countries we have been sending missionaries to would start sending missionaries back to us.

It's here! About 20% of all American priests (31% of seminarians) now are foreign-born. In January, we started our new "World Priest" program at Saint Meinrad to help international priests acclimate and adjust to American culture and to help parishioners adjust to them.

I have written about this phenomenon several times. Today I want to offer an encouraging word to our native-born priests who are serving as missionaries overseas and here in what we call the "home missions."

The Document on Bishops from Vatican Council II said this: "As far as possible, bishops should arrange for some of their own priests to go to the missions to exercise the sacred ministry permanently or at least for a set period of time."

Maybe this is a good time to remind ourselves that two of our diocesan priests are serving in the missions abroad, and three are serving in the "southern Kentucky missions." This does not include locally born priests and sisters who are members of religious orders, nor lay persons who work in programs like the Jesuit Volunteer Corps, nor pastors who have "mission churches" attached to their parishes around the diocese.

Our own Father Joe Hayden has been serving faithfully in parishes in Peru for many years. My classmate, Father Charlie Dittmeier, has been ministering as a Maryknoll associate to deaf communities in places like Cambodia for as many years.

Fathers Dan Whelan, Larry Gelthaus and Kevin Bryan represent us in the Southern Kentucky Missions. Many others, including myself, have been fortunate enough to have had those assignments as priests. More religious sisters and lay people than I can recall have served with them. Many more of our priests, sisters and laity serve a variety of "mission" churches that are attached to established parishes around the diocese.

One of biggest losers in the shortage of priests and religious has been in the area of evangelization. It is interesting to note that when the Vatican II Document on Priests says that priests have as their primary duty the proclamation of the gospel to all, it says first to unbelievers and second to the faithful. It would be a shame to think that we can no longer afford to proclaim the gospel to unbelievers because of the needs of the faithful.

To all our missionaries, we offer a word of encouragement and a well-deserved "thank you" for your sacrifices. You make us proud.

*April 28, 2011*

# Are You Willing to Die for Your Faith?

*We are ready to die rather than transgress the laws of our ancestors. II Maccabees 7:2*

When I was a teenaged seminarian out at the now-closed St. Thomas Seminary on old Brownsboro Road, we used to come into the dining room for lunch in silence, standing at our assigned seats until everybody was assembled before we sat down at table together. Before we started eating, we used to listen to one of the other seminarians read a story of one of the martyrs who had given his life for the faith. Every day we heard about courageous men, women and even children who had their heads or hands chopped off, who had been boiled in oil, shot full of arrows, hanged or crucified rather than abandon their faith.

Often, as I sat there listening, I wondered whether I would have the courage to lay down my life for the faith in such a situation or whether I would lie to my torturers' faces in an attempt to save my own life. I don't like pain. Honestly, I am a little skeptical about whether I could hold out for very long.

The reading cited above is one of my favorite Old Testament readings. It is about character, integrity, principle and courage. It is about a saintly Jewish mother and her seven courageous sons who were forced to choose between their religious principles and expediency. They were forced to choose between what would get them ahead for the moment and what would get them ahead in the long run.

Talking about a story about character, integrity, principle and courage! This woman not only watched all of her children be tortured and killed right before her eyes, she even egged them on before she herself was killed along with them. This has to be one of the best hero stories in all of Scripture.

Would you be willing to die for your Catholic faith? Sadly, most of us wouldn't these days. We do not live in a culture where character, integrity, principle or courage are generally valued. We live in a culture of expediency, the "latest best offer" and "being served on demand." Many of us do not think in terms of dying for our faith, but making sure our faith does not get in the way of our living.

Many of us today do not want to change our lives so that they conform to the teachings of the church. Instead, we want the church to change its teachings to fit the way we live our lives. Instead of being loyal to our parishes and help them become life-giving, we shop for a better offer. Instead of seeing the church as a place for us to serve others, we expect it to be a place where we are served. How could we ever hope to die for our faith when we don't even want our faith to inconvenience us?

People of principle do the right thing, inconvenient or not.

*May 5, 2011*

# Sharing Personal Stories Can Be Gratifying

*I say again what I have said before. Galatians 1:9*

One of the things about getting older is the tendency to repeat oneself. I plead guilty! I do it sometimes by accident at the seminary when I forget that I have told the same story more than once in a semester to my class of deacons. Other times I do it on purpose as part of a homily when I relate a personal experience that I had years ago. For the former, I apologize. For the latter, I don't!

Recently, a seminarian was telling one of my brother priests about a homily I gave in the seminary chapel and how much he liked the opening story. That priest's sarcastic response was, "Oh, he's been singing that old song since he was ordained!" (We priests can be very hard on each other.) At first, I was embarrassed that maybe I do repeat some of my stories too often. After fretting about it for a while, I concluded that I won't stop telling my stories, because I know from experience that every time I tell them somebody there is helped by the telling of them whether my audience is familiar or not.

I recently agreed to meet with a man over coffee who had attended a parish mission I had preached. Because I have had only one life, I had to retell a couple of my old "recovery" stories. He was moved enough to ask to meet with me about "coming back to church." Those old stories seem to appeal especially to marginal, disaffected and non-practicing Catholics.

On one hand, nobody wants to hear about how bad somebody else has had it. On the other hand, however, many do want to know how others have overcome distressing situations similar to theirs. The baseball player, Johnny Sain, put it succinctly when he said, "Nobody wants to hear about the labor pains; they just want to see the baby!" Helen Keller said as much when she wrote, "Although the world is full of suffering, it is full also of the overcoming of it." Her fame comes not from her disabilities, but from her overcoming them.

What makes the sharing of stories work is when they start with the status quo, have some conflict or challenge that must be overcome or resolved, and end with a different status quo in which something has changed, something new has been learned or some problem has been solved.

Given the right opportunity, sharing such stories with others can be a gratifying experience for those who listen as well as a therapeutic experience for the one doing the telling. Even though each of us has lived through different experiences, we all have common threads that run through our lives. Faith can be shared. Seeds can be planted. Lives can be touched. God can be glorified.

As one of my friends often reminds me when we talk about this subject, "What is most personal is most universal."

*May 12, 2011*

# The Church Needs Imagination and Ideas

*Behold, I make all things new! Revelation 21:5*

One of my favorite books is "The Art of Possibility." It is part of a small collection of books I have assembled on the subject of "imaginative thinking." Even though it is not a religious book, it reinforces a belief I have had for a long time that the biggest shortage in the Catholic Church may just be imagination. Bob Dylan used to sing, "If you are not busy being born, you are busy dying."

We have so much going for us, and yet we don't seem to be able to "offer new generations, through the believable proclamation of the Gospel, ever new reasons of life and hope," as Pope Benedict put it in his April General Intention.

Statistically, one of the major reasons for Catholics "dropping out" is not church teaching or even the sexual abuse scandal, but boredom. That boredom is not so much with what we have to offer as it is with how we offer it. We need a new birth of imagination — akin to the imagination our spiritual ancestors had when they started most of our struggling institutions.

With a lot of readings this time of year about the growth of the early church, I am reminded of an idea that I have had on my mind for years. I am sure there are plenty of people out there who are more than willing to point out why this would not work, but that has never stopped me from presenting my ideas. Some of them, of course, have been shot down immediately. Some have germinated for some time before sprouting later. Still others have lain dormant till a more acceptable presenter has come forward, making that idea more palatable.

We need a non-geographical parish that specializes in evangelistic preaching, powerful music and adult education, a parish whose mission it is to reach out to fallen-away Catholics in such a way as to "get them back on their feet" and "feed them back into our local parishes." These parishioners "graduate."

This new "parish" would be staffed by "missionaries" from around the diocese who would commit to a few years of service: two or three of our best preachers, some top-notch music ministers and liturgy specialists, and several of our best faith formation ministers. There would be no service committees. Members would be encouraged to contribute to, and become involved in, already existing service programs in the community or in other parishes.

In the Catholic Church, we have a whole range of smart people with ideas of their own, but we do not always give them a regular platform to share their ideas. Why couldn't we structure an "idea fair" and encourage our people to bring original ideas related to a full range of ministries? The deal would be that nobody had to accept any ideas, but even a "not-so-good idea" just might trigger "the best idea ever," an idea that could work.

*May 19, 2011*

# Taking Responsibility For One's Faith

*We no longer believe because of your word, for we have heard for ourselves. John 4:42*

The famous Soren Kierkegaard, Danish philosopher and theologian (1813-1855), is known for his famous story of the clown and the burning village, which describes pretty well the predicament of those of us who have been given the "primary task" of preaching the word of God in today's culture.

According to the story, a traveling circus in Denmark caught fire. The manager sent the clown, already dressed and made up for the performance, into the town to get help and to warn the people that the fire was spreading across fields of dry rubble toward them.

The clown ran into the village and screamed for help, but the people thought it was a publicity stunt, so they applauded and laughed. The clown tried in vain to get the people to be serious and to come help put out the fire. The more he pleaded, the more they laughed and clapped. Finally, it was too late for help. The fire engulfed the circus and burned the village to the ground.

We clerics, religious and lay ministers are that "clown," dressed in our funny clothes, trying to get people to listen to our life-saving message, but we find that people are taking us and our vital message less and less seriously.

After Vatican II, some thought that people would listen to us if we would only take off our make-up, don secular vocabulary and change our costumes. Now there are those who think that we can make things all right once more if we just put all that back on again. One of the most pressing problems facing Catholicism may be the fact that we are unable to influence our culture to take our message seriously, no matter how vital we may think it is.

One problem may be that we tend to be too institutionally focused, rather than focused on life as it is lived by the faithful. The agendas of bishops, priests and seminarians — and even permanent deacons and career church workers, for that matter — are often not the agendas of the laity.

Here is another problem. Since we can no longer impose unquestioned rules on the behavior of the laity, we tend to blame them for their lack of faith and the culture for its secularism and moral relativism. Instead, we need to own our own inability to influence them to move from where they are to where God wants them to be. In a consumer society, we have to be able to navigate around the obstacles and become more skillful in getting our message across. We have to become convincing.

A final problem is the fact that many of our members have not absorbed a fundamental teaching of Vatican II — that they can no longer abdicate their responsibility to live as mature Christian adults to the clergy and that we can no longer be a church of children led by surrogate parents.

*May 26, 2011*

# Advice to Graduates

*My prayer is that you may be able to discern what is of value. Philippians 1*

It's graduation season — time for old people to give advice to captive audiences of young people. Since I have been involved with the graduates of Bellarmine University and Saint Meinrad School of Theology, I thought I would share some of the advice I have tried to offer them with you, the readers of this column. I offered them a challenge and a prayer.

My challenge is to grab the bull by the horns, to take responsibility for themselves and their actions, to stand up to the lazy coward within them and discipline themselves to do hard things for their own good. This challenge can best be summed up in two of my favorite quotes from George Bernard Shaw.

In speaking about living on purpose, rather than by accident, Shaw said, first of all, "Life is not about finding yourself. Life is about creating yourself." Next, Shaw said, "This is the true joy in life ... the being a force of nature instead of a feverish, selfish little clod of ailments and grievances, complaining that the world will not devote itself to making you happy."

My prayer for them is found in the reading cited above, in Saint Paul's Letter to the Christian community of Philippi. "May you be able to discern what is of value!" Like the citizens of Philippi — a great commercial center, a crossroads — where every idea, custom and habit imaginable competed for acceptance, they too are blessed to live in a world where every idea, custom and habit competes for their acceptance — some good and some bad.

One of the benefits of being a young adult is finally being able to enjoy the freedom to choose. One of the up sides of the freedom to choose is the possibility of building one's own life the way one wants it through a series of well-thought-out choices. One of the down sides of the freedom to choose is the possibility of ruining one's own life through a series of poorly-thought-out choices.

Some graduates can handle freedom. They are able to discern what is of value and choose it, parlaying it into an incredible life. Others cannot handle freedom. They are unable to discern what is of value, choosing only what feels good in the moment, and end up forced to live in a self-created hell of regret.

Graduates, today is your day! "Carpe diem — Seize the day!"

Be a force of nature, not a complaining little clod of grievances and ailments.

"Discern what is of value" and develop the self-discipline to grab onto it. Do not be like the maiden and the judge, living in regret in Whittier's poem Maude Miller, of whom it was said: "For of all sad words of tongue or pen, the saddest of these: "It might have been!"

Know that freedom and responsibility go together. Choose freedom and the responsibility that goes with it.

*June 2, 2011*

# Looking Toward Retirement

*Can any of you by worrying add a single moment to your life span? Matthew 6:27*

The retirement clock started ticking when I began receiving those incessant mailings from AARP around my fifty-fifth birthday — the ones I disposed of with rubber gloves as if they were tainted with anthrax.

Those indignities were soon followed by a stream of well-meaning young women who asked me, unsolicited, if I wanted the "senior coffee" to go with my McDonald's sausage biscuit.

Over the last twelve years, those humiliations have begun to come in an increasingly steady stream of warnings that it is time to sign up for Medicare, invitations to order my own "chair" from the Scooter Store (at no cost to me) and threats that I need to "act now before it's too late" to get in on a funeral policy program to cover the costs of my "final arrangements."

I still can't seem to get around to updating that file that the Chancery sent me a few months ago that includes my funeral plans. I can't even go to the airport without being confronted with "terminal" and "departure" signs everywhere I look. Even my doctor wants to see me twice a year now. (I always wonder if he knows something I don't know?)

The retirement clock is ticking even louder these days. Maybe it's the fact that I just reached my sixty-seventh birthday; maybe it's because "remote retirement planning" was a topic in my "transition from seminary and into ministry" class that I just concluded at Saint Meinrad. Maybe it's because I just got another one of those "this is what you will get when you retire" schedules from the Social Security Administration.

But any way you cut the cake, I have about three years to go before retirement. With the "facts" staring me in the face, the only delusions of youth left are those periodic "Oh, you certainly don't look your age" comments that sympathetic people toss my way. Pathetically, I find myself lapping them up more and more, like a needy puppy. I always thought old age was for other people.

"If you don't laugh, you cry!" Actually, I am laughing as I write this column. I hope you realize that much of this has been tongue in cheek, because at this point in my life I know I have been blessed. In fact, I actually look forward to creating, with God's help, a "second career" within my priesthood. What I hope to do over the next three years, before I retire from the Institute for Priests and Presbyterates, is to design and pilot a new comprehensive "priest retirement program," one that would focus on a more imaginative and creative use of our retired priests than what we have presently.

To all those my age and older, let the words of Blessed John Paul II be our motto: "Remember the past with gratitude, live the present with enthusiasm and look forward to the future with confidence."

*June 9, 2011*

# Religion Should Bind People Together

*Whoever says he is in the light, yet hates his brother, is still in the darkness. I John 2:9*

There is a lot of meanness emanating from so-called "religious" people. It's probably no more prevalent than in the past, but today Internet social networking technology and the TV talk-show phenomenon have given these angry people instant and cheap access to millions so that they can spew their venom freely.

Some, who present themselves as "super-Catholics" (or, as we used to say, "more Catholic than the Pope") are some of the worst. Their blogs leave my jaw dropped in horror. Sometimes their target is a lay person, sometimes a nun, sometimes a priest, often a bishop and sometimes even the Pope himself.

Nevermind that their hero, Blessed John Paul II, spoke often about the necessity of being "men of communion" and that "legitimate diversity" is to be respected. (The worst of the worst do not even recognize John Paul II as a "true" Pope.) Nevermind that the U.S. Catholic bishops have had to issue a pastoral letter on civility in the media condemning such vitriol. Nevermind that one of Jesus' most important tenets was "to offer no resistance to injury," "to love your enemies" and to "pray for those who persecute you." "It is not those who say 'Lord, Lord,' but those who do the will of my Father!"

My hunch is that there is, more often than not, a personality disorder being manifested, not purely a passionate love for God and his church, as they would have their listeners and readers believe. Simply being angry does not necessarily make one a "prophet." The word "religion" has its origins in the Latin *"re-ligare,"* meaning "to bind things together," "to restore opposites to each other." Is not the most basic role of religion, then, to "bring differences together as one?"

According to a new in-depth survey, seventy-six percent of those polled said that places of worship are "very responsible" or "somewhat responsible" for improving civility in America. How can we be credible "men of communion" in an epidemic of enemy making unless we are "religious" in the truest sense — unless we have the ability to *"re-ligare"* — to help people manage their differences?

"I have heard it said that heroism can be redefined for our age as the ability to tolerate paradox, to embrace seemingly opposing forces without rejecting one or the other just for the sheer relief of it, and to understand that life is the game played between two paradoxical goalposts: winning is good and so is losing; freedom is good and so is authority; having and giving; action and passivity; sex and celibacy; income and outgo; courage and fear. Both are true. They may sit on opposite sides of the table, but underneath it their legs are entwined." (*CALLINGS*, Gregg Levoy, p. 53.)

Pope Paul VI said, "Dialogue is a recognized method of the apostolate. However divergent views may be, they can often serve to complete each other."

June 16, 2011

# A Salute to Siblings

*How good it is, how pleasant, where brothers and sisters dwell as one! Psalm 133:1*

Every Christmas, I get together with my four sisters, two brothers and three brothers-in-law. We always begin with Mass, remembering our parents and various other family members who have died. At the end, we remind ourselves that we cannot always assume that we will all be together again next year. We conclude with a big meal around a single table, retelling the same stories from childhood that we have told every year before.

I always look forward to it because we all "get along" amazingly well! I used to naively think that everyone's family was like that, but after 41 years of priesthood, I now know better. I know that many families cannot gather because of old hurts or hearts that have grown cold from neglect.

Today, I would like to salute my own siblings in hopes that those of you reading this may take the time to reach out and affirm your own, especially those with whom you have not had much contact for a while or those from whom you may be estranged.

My sister, Brenda, has had to bear that sense of responsibility that seems to go with being the oldest. She has a strong sense of duty that has driven her to work hard all her life. She is often the first one there in time of need. She has had to handle her share of tragedies. She is resilient and generous.

After me came my brother Gary. Gary is more like our grandfather, Leo, who was cool and patient. He, too, has been a hard worker who has tended to think of the needs of others before his own.

Lois is most like my mother, generous to a fault. She is the one who looks for those little things she can do to bring people a bit of happiness. She has my great grandmother's love for travel. She could have been a flight attendant, traveling and waiting on people at the same time.

Nancy has my father's drive and my mother's heart. She is the family's "Energizer Bunny." She just keeps on going and going and going. She, too, is selfless to a fault. She feels other people's pain like no one else I know.

Kaye is the mother of three boys. In a man's world, and being the youngest girl in the family, she has had to learn to stand up for herself. All that has made her disciplined and organized, and it has given her a great sense of humor as well.

Mark, the youngest, and I inherited our father's unrelenting drive to accomplish. Our motto is "Anything worth doing is worth overdoing." As much as that might drive us to the point of exhaustion at times, probably neither of us would have it any other way.

If you say you love your siblings, why not tell them? It won't hurt you and it could help them.

*June 23, 2011*

# Creating Yourself Takes Courage

*You have taken off the old self and put on the new self, which is being renewed. Colossians 3: 9, 10*

With book 16 at the press, I have started a 17th! The one I am working on now is another one for priests, entitled **Molding Yourself Into the Priest You Are Called to Be: Self Formation in Priestly Formation**. I got the idea from Blessed Pope John Paul II: "All formation, priestly formation included, is ultimately self formation."

I would like to share one of those principles, because I think it applies to more than priests. I believe that this principle applies to all of us. We have more power to create the selves we want to be than we know.

As you look at your own life, which of the following statements is more true?

"Life is something that happens to you, and all you can do is make the most of it."

"Life is not about finding yourself; life is about creating yourself."

"Do you feel more like a passenger in someone else's car or the driver behind the wheel of your own?"

"Do you feel you have the bull by the horns or that you are being dragged by it?"

I do believe that some people have had more advantages, opportunities and luck than others, but I also believe that we have more power than we know to be more than we are, regardless of advantages, opportunities or luck. How else can we account for those who have overcome great obstacles to rise to great heights and those who have crashed and burned from the heights of great advantage, opportunity and luck?

We are more powerful than we know in creating the lives we want, as long as we get over our belief in magic, as long as we quit clinging conveniently to a sense of victimhood and as long as we stand up to our own lazy cowardice. Even when we have lost everything, even when we are dying from a terminal illness, we are still powerful, because we can always choose how we want to respond to it.

Self-creation takes courage, and because it takes courage, we often sabotage our own success because it makes life less difficult, less risky, less scary and less threatening.

Often we are held back by the beliefs about ourselves that we have come to accept or have absorbed from others. With low self-esteem, we avoid being powerful, and we unconsciously choose to be helpless. We withdraw from the simplest demands in a task, as well as from life's opportunities.

Feeling powerless, we want to be taken care of. We look for strong people to lean on and upon whom we can be dependent. We become "feverish little clods of grievances and ailments, complaining that the world will not get together to make us happy." We are afraid to admit that much of what we hate about our lives is the result of a long series of lazy choices over a lifetime.

*June 30, 2011*

# Live Simply to Live Well

*Forsake foolishness that you may live.*
*Proverbs 9:6*

The present financial crisis is a true dilemma for many. Dilemma, meaning "two horns," has traditionally stood for "crisis" and "opportunity." I would like to explore the "opportunity" that this "crisis" provides.

Living well does not necessarily depend on having more money or things. If we don't have enough money, there are two things we can do: increase our income or simplify our lives. Since many of us do not have the option of increasing our income significantly, simplifying our lives may be our most realistic option.

Instead of looking at this option as a cross to bear, why not look at it as an exciting challenge that requires imagination? A good example of this is the "coupon queen" I saw on TV recently who goes home regularly with several hundred dollars' worth of groceries for only a few dollars of actual money.

Voluntary simplicity involves both internal and external choices. It involves the internal decision for honesty and clarity of purpose as well as the external decision to avoid clutter and complication irrelevant to living well. This means partial restraint in one area of our lives so as to have greater abundance in another.

**Where we live** — The Shakers did not have a lot of time to waste on displaying and cleaning knick-knacks and layered decorations. Their designs were not only clean and simple, but also efficient. While my house is not that "Shaker," I do like to "keep it simple." That not only saves money, but even more so, time. I go through my house once a year and de-clutter it.

**What we wear** — I like nice clothes, simple clothes, quality clothes, clothes that last. So that it doesn't cost an arm and a leg, I never buy clothes in season or trendy clothes. I buy summer clothes in the fall and winter clothes in the spring — things that never go out of style.

**What we eat** — I battle my weight more than my budget, but lately I have found a way to do both. During the summer especially, I like to stir-fry fresh vegetables and lean meat in a wok. I can eat as much as I like. I can fill up without guilt. It is healthy. It is cheap. It is fast and easy.

**Where we vacation** — I like to vacation at home. I plan it out. I like to sleep late, cook for friends, eat out, visit people I haven't visited in a long time and take advantage of local entertainment. It is stress-free and very inexpensive. If I "go somewhere," I like to spend a few extra days at places where I have to travel anyway.

At the seminary, I actually teach young priests-to-be how to live well on less so that they can get out of debt quickly and save more for retirement. Sometimes, living well is more about imagination, creativity and invention than it is about money.

*July 7, 2011*

# A Time To Laugh

*There is a time to weep and a time to laugh.*
*Ecclesiastes 3:4*

At a time when nothing seems funny in the church anymore, I thought these stories might make you smile.

Cardinal Alfredo Ottaviani, a tenacious watchdog of orthodoxy, was a major defender of the status quo at the Second Vatican Council. One story from Vatican II days had him hopping into a Roman taxicab and exclaiming to the driver, "Take me to the Council!" His reputation solidly entrenched in people's minds, the driver headed for the city of Trent (the scene of a council 400 years before).

When Bishop Carroll Dozier became Bishop of Memphis, Tenn., in 1971, he soon scheduled a general-absolution ceremony in a sports arena. Some 14,000 showed up.

Rome did not approve of general absolution except for emergency circumstances, such as existed in battle areas during World War II. Bishop Dozier blamed Cardinal Spellman of New York when he was summoned to Rome to appear before the Congregation for Divine Worship and Discipline of the Sacraments to be reproved and directed not to repeat the ceremony.

When Bishop Dozier's plane circled New York in preparation for landing, an unchastened Bishop Dozier joshed to a friend, "I looked out the window, raised my right hand and absolved the whole city of New York — everyone, that is, except Cardinal Spellman!"

When Cardinal Sarto of Venice was elected Pope Pius X, he had pawned all his personal possessions to help the poor. When it came time for him to appear on the balcony overlooking St. Peter's Square after his election as pope, all he had was a cheap tin cross, because he had pawned his silver episcopal cross. Some were troubled, but not the new pope. "No one will notice. It looks quite like the real thing!"

Most people have heard Pope John XXIII's most famous joke. He was showing a visitor around the Vatican one day, and the visitor asked how many persons worked there. "About half," Pope John replied.

Cardinal Cushing of Boston was famous for his small regard for pomp and circumstance. At confirmation ceremonies, he would pace about and ask those to be confirmed questions from the catechism. He posed easy questions and glossed over blunders.

At one such ceremony, Cardinal Cushing came across Michael Cronin, son of Joe Cronin, then manager of the Boston Red Sox. "Who made the world?" Cardinal Cushing asked Michael. "God made the world," said Michael. "Who made the Red Sox?" Cardinal Cushing countered. "Tom Yawkey," declared the youth, citing the then-current owner of the Red Sox. Cardinal Cushing waited for the laughter to subside, then said: "You certainly know your catechism!"

Bishop Sheen, a great fund raiser for the missions, liked to tell the story of a young girl who was hugely successful raising money for the missions. Many of her customers returned three or four times. Her mother asked her where she was getting all the lemonade. The girl answered, "From the cocktail shaker you had in the icebox."

*July 14, 2011*

# Forgiveness Brings Freedom

*A wound can be bandaged and an insult forgiven.*
*Sirach 27:21*

I read that Amazon.com lists 160,510 books on the topic of forgiveness. That's 31,629 more than on sexuality. What does that tell us about the human heart and what it hungers for most?

You haven't experienced freedom unless you have experienced the freedom that comes when you let go of resentments that sear your soul, preoccupy your thoughts and drain your strength. Yet, there are so many people who hug their hurts and nurse their wounds in an all-consuming preoccupation because they cannot "let go."

When they refuse to forgive, they choose to be "right" over being free. Catherine Ponder said it best when she said, "When you hold resentment toward another, you are bound to that person by an emotional link that is stronger than steel. Forgiveness is the only way to dissolve that link and get free."

The biggest mistake people make when it comes to forgiveness is to believe that it is a favor one does for the one who has wronged them. It was Suzanne Somers who said it best when she said, "Forgiveness is a gift you give yourself."

Lewis B. Smedes said it this way: "To forgive is to set a prisoner free and discover that the prisoner was you." Alan Paton pointed out, "When deep injury is done us, we never recover until we forgive."

Another mistake people make when it comes to forgiveness is to believe that forgiveness is a sign of weakness and spinelessness if you don't "stand up for yourself." Actually, as Mohandas Gandhi pointed out, "The weak can never forgive. Forgiveness is the attribute of the strong."

The refusal to forgive keeps one imprisoned in the past. Paul Boese put it this way: "Forgiveness does not change the past, but it does enlarge the future." Archbishop Desmund Tutu of South Africa said, "Without forgiveness, there is no future." Forgiveness is basically a choice to have a future over a past.

The biggest obstacle of all to forgiveness is the belief that the one who wrongs you needs to apologize, make amends and show evidence of change. While that is certainly part of justice, it is not essential.

Forgiveness is most powerful when it is unilateral and unconditional. Unilateral and unconditional forgiveness is a sign of ultimate strength, because when you forgive unilaterally, you take charge of your situation and refuse to be someone else's victim any longer.

I have been a priest for 41 years. I can honestly say that the most spiritual experience of my life was not the day I was ordained, not the day I said my first Mass, baptized my first baby, married my first couple, anointed my own mother before she died or presided at my first funeral. The most spiritual experience of my life was the day I decided consciously to forgive and seek forgiveness. I finally realized that taking offense is just as toxic as giving offense.

*July 21, 2011*

# Choosing To Be Catholic

*Should anyone ask you for the reason for this hope of yours, be ever ready to reply, but speak gently and respectfully. I Peter 3:15*

It started back in the very beginning of my ministry — being challenged by people who want to know why I would choose to be a Catholic. It has been a constant in my 41 years of priesthood.

Some choose public situations to attack verbally. Some soften the blow by making their discounting comments from behind a mask of humor. Others ask their question calmly and respectfully, in all sincerity.

The first angry attack came at one of the receptions held in my honor right after ordination. The first "put-down" came from an angry ex-Catholic who wanted to stake out what he obviously thought was "higher ground" than the ground I was standing on. The first calm and respectful question came from a Catholic who wanted to believe, but was struggling to hang on.

Actually, I would credit these people with strengthening my faith more than shaking it, bringing it more into focus than those who blindly accept everything just because their religious teachers said so. By challenging my faith, they have made it stronger — like gold in a furnace.

The same thing happened when I was the Vocation Director. For seven solid years, I was forced to defend priesthood to people who were not convinced of its value or its sustainability in the future. Often, I felt like I was trying to sell tickets to the Titanic. My confidence was shaken more than once, but in the end my conviction about the priesthood did not crumble; it became stronger — like tempered steel.

"That which doesn't kill you, makes you stronger" (Friedrich Nietzsche). "Adversity has the effect of eliciting talents which, in prosperous circumstances, would have lain dormant" (Horace). "Truth often suffers more by the heat of its defenders than from the arguments of its opposers" (William Penn).

Nobody knows how many Catholics have "left the kitchen" because they "couldn't take the heat." I do not judge them. Many of them are still my friends. Some, I am convinced, left because they spent more time looking for reasons to leave than looking for reasons to stay.

There are many "good" reasons to leave the priesthood, even leave the church, but I attribute my staying not to my superior faith, but simply because I have spent a lot more time looking for reasons to stay than reasons to go.

Today, there is probably more stuff in print supporting reasons to leave than reasons to stay, but there are still a couple of good books out there I can recommend — both by Michael Leach. One is called "I Like Being Catholic: Treasured Traditions, Rituals and Stories," and the other one, a newer one, is called "Why Stay Catholic?: Unexpected Answers to a Life-Changing Question."

Stay in or get out? I believe much depends on where you place your focus.

*July 28, 2011*

# Demographic of Priests is Changing

*You are no longer strangers and sojourners.*
*Ephesians 2:19*

"The times they are a-changin'," sang Bob Dylan in 1964. Almost fifty years later, they are still "a-changin,'" and there is even more change on the horizon.

After conducting more than 100 priest assemblies, convocations, retreats and study days in six countries, two things have stood out.

First, we are aging as a group. In spite of the recent spike in seminarians, the room is usually dominated by "gray hairs." I have heard that 50 percent of all American priests will retire in the next ten years. If that is true, it saddens, scares and worries me.

Second, we are becoming more internationalized. It is common to look out over a room full of priests and see that they are from everywhere — places such as Vietnam, the Philippines, Nigeria, Poland, Mexico, Kenya, India, El Salvador and Indonesia.

The "seniorization" of the U.S. clergy is new, but the "internationalization" of the U.S. clergy is not. In 1886, 30 of the 47 U.S. bishops were foreign-born. Even the early pastors of my home parish in Rhodelia were from Belgium, France, Holland, Luxemburg, Germany and Ireland.

By the time I started seminary in 1958, American missionary orders like Maryknoll and the Passionists were sending many missionaries to Africa, Asia and South America. Halfway through the seminary, I was reading predictions that we would someday see that the places where we sent missionaries would be sending them back to us.

Sixteen of the 64 priests in the Diocese of Victoria, Texas, are from Ghana. I was recently in the Diocese of Little Rock and found that around a dozen of their priests are from Nigeria. When I was speaking in San Francisco, I was surprised to know that one-fourth of the pastors are Filipino.

One African bishop summarized it best. "I am excited that my country can provide Catholic priests to serve as missionaries in other countries facing a priest shortage because it is a way to repay the West for fostering the church in Ghana. The church in the West is our mother church because they gave us birth, planted the faith and sacrificed lives. It's time for us to return the compliment. It's not that we don't need them. I could open three parishes now, but we make the sacrifice so that the faith and ministry may go on here in the United States."

I know that this is not a real solution to our problems, but I'm hopeful it will wake us up to the facts that are staring us in the face.

I am open to about any legitimate solution but one. There seem to be some who would like to run off enough of our members and trim the church severely until it fits available "orthodox" clergy. That scares me to death.

In the meantime, I will continue to work with Saint Meinrad in our new World Priest Program and try to orient international priests to American parishes and American parishioners to international priests.

*August 4, 2011*

# Children Have Religious Experiences

*Unless you turn and become like children, you will not enter the kingdom of heaven. Matthew 18:3*

Children do have religious experiences. I know this from my own reading, and I know it from my own personal experience.

One of the most fascinating spiritual people I have ever encountered was a little boy by the name of Mattie J. T. Stepanek, who died of a rare neuromuscular disease in 2004. At age three he began to compose poetry, which he called "heartsongs." By the time he died at fourteen, he had seven New York Bestseller books. His poetry is "spiritual" in the deepest sense of the word. I have seen him being interviewed several times on TV, and I own three of his books of poetry. He had the inner strength to look beyond his medical and physical challenges to provide millions with a positive and wonderful perspective on life.

I was reminded of Mattie Stepanek when I was driving through Stephensport, Kentucky, last spring on my way from Saint Meinrad to my home town in Rhodelia. As I drove past the little white-sided Stephensport Baptist Church, I was suddenly reminded of one of my first religious experiences. I do not remember how old I was, but I clearly remember the experience.

In that church, I attended the funeral of one of my mother's uncles, "Pole" Chappell. I can still remember that it was rare for us Catholics to darken the doorway of a Protestant Church.

It was considered a sin unless you "had" to go because of a family member. If we did, we were warned not to "participate," but to sit there. I can remember my dear mother, who tried to follow the rules of the Church, instructing us before we entered not to sing or answer the prayers.

I can still remember clearly thinking to myself during the service that I was not supposed to "like" their lively preaching and spirited music. I also remember flirting with sin and "liking" it anyway. I remember my "outsides" being very still while my "insides" were dancing! It was there that I had my first memorable religious experience.

I stopped in front of the Stephensport Baptist Church that day, took a picture with my cell phone camera and tried to remember as much of that experience as possible. I remembered that my mother's uncle was buried on a hill near the church beside a big cedar tree. It did not take me more than a few minutes to see a sign to a hilltop cemetery overlooking the town. Getting out of my car, I practically walked straight to the grave. There it was after all these years! It told me that I had just turned seven years old, because the tombstone read, "Harvey N. ("Pole" was short for Napoleon) Chappell, died August 7, 1951."

I know that we forget more than we remember, but I believe that some of our most memorable experiences are our religious experiences, even those from childhood.

*August 18, 2011*

# Three Phases of Spiritual Growth

*I was once a blasphemer and a persecutor and an arrogant man. I acted out of ignorance in my unbelief. I Timothy 1:13*

Paul's admission to the sin of obnoxious certainty has always fascinated me because it is one of the most predictable sins of those on fire with new spiritual enthusiasm.

Paul admits to this sin in his letter to the young missionary, Timothy, quoted above. Paul might have been trying to warn Timothy, in his youthful enthusiasm, about being obnoxiously certain in ministry.

He reminds Timothy that before his conversion, he himself had been so sure, certain and convinced in his need to protect the old-time religion that he was willing to have Christians corralled and killed. He calls himself "an arrogant blasphemer and persecutor."

Thomas Merton, the famous Trappist monk, knew of this arrogance as well. He admits to God in his famous prayer, "The fact that I think I am following your will does not mean that I am actually doing so."

As I go around the country speaking to priests about being spiritual leaders, I often talk about three stages that people typically go through in spiritual growth: an entry event, an exploration phase and, finally, an integration period.

The second stage is often marked by obnoxious certainty. In the entry phase one is introduced to a new idea, insight or program. The exploration phase is often so empowering that it can become intoxicating. It may be the first Medjugorje pilgrimage, Charismatic meeting, Marriage Encounter program, A.A. or Al-Anon meeting or weekend monastery retreat.

In the parish, those in this phase are the people who regularly show up at the parish office on Mondays when they get home from these experiences and insist that the whole parish must go through the same experiences immediately. It is a period of "obnoxious certainty."

Peter had one of these experiences on the mountain of transfiguration. What he experienced was so powerful and intoxicating that he said to Jesus, "Let us build three tents and stay up here forever!" These "peak experiences" are wonderful, and they offer us an entry into spiritual growth, but they are often followed by a fall before they are truly integrated.

Even though Jesus warned Peter that they had to go down the mountain to face suffering and death, Peter would hear none of it. He bragged that even if everybody were to abandon Jesus, he himself would be willing to die for him. As Jesus was being led to the cross, it was Peter who said, "Jesus who? I don't think I have ever heard of him!"

Humility may be the most needed and, often, the least obvious virtue to be found in those new to the spiritual life. When we are most certain, we need to be most scared. Like Paul, the day we think we know it all is the day we are "cruisin' for a bruisin."

With humility, we can arrive in time at a third phase — integration.

*August 25, 2011*

# "Why Are People Mean?"

*He is so mean that no one can talk to him.*
*I Samuel 25:17*

As a follow up to last week's column and last summer's "debt debates," and in light of today's anniversary of our infamous 9-11 attack, I would like to say a few words about a growing phenomenon — "meanness."

As I noted last week, writing can actually be hazardous to one's health. While it is true that ninety-nine percent of the feedback I get (at least to my face) is very positive, I have gotten my share of pretty mean responses. The negative responses range from ridicule and outright attack to "bombs" wrapped in humor. Being a writer is a lot like being on the "Gong Show."

Here's how I handle caustic criticism. If I have never heard a positive comment from them, I tend to chalk it up to the fact that I have triggered some pain going on inside them. If they have been generous in affirming me for something in the past, then I tend to take to heart what they are saying and look for the problem residing in me.

There is a lot of meanness going around today — most of it much more serious than what I have reported above. Years ago, John Steinbeck may have summarized our world today when he said that we admire kindness, generosity, openness, honesty, understanding and feeling, but we know that sharpness, greed, acquisitiveness, meanness, egotism and self-interest work. Being nice is now associated with failure, while being mean is associated with success.

I don't know about you, but my first response to meanness is to be mean back! My second response is to take the poison in and let my wound get infected. My third and best response (when I am strong spiritually and emotionally) is to try to not take it in, but to keep it "out there" until I can understand it.

Why are people mean? Meanness seems to be an attempt at domination by people who believe that they have been hurt, that they have no power and that their pain may return again. It is a way for the mean person to try to diminish the power of the person he or she is being mean to and, therefore, gain that power. It's a rush, almost like a drug — "Look how miserable I can make this person."

The secret to diffusing the situation is to refuse to "bite" (or, as Jesus put it, "turn the other cheek"), thereby not granting the sought-after "payoff." This takes an incredible amount of self-confidence, self-discipline and spiritual maturity.

The question I like to ask myself when I feel attacked by mean people is, "What is the problem behind this problem?" I try to identify the hurting in the one being mean and try to heal it. If I cannot, I try to resolve to say nothing — what I call "not hitting the ball back over the net." When I do that, the game is usually over pretty quickly.

*September 1, 2011*

# Self-Control Takes Practice

*The spirit is willing, but the flesh is weak.*
*Matthew 26:41*

One of the TV shows that I get seduced into watching is "Locked Up Abroad." It is a series about people who are caught trying to smuggle large amounts of illegal drugs into the United States from Asian or South American countries. Those arrested are not the hardened criminal types, but bright, educated and law-abiding young men or women, usually financially strapped, who are faced with an opportunity to step out of character for a moment and decide to take unbelievable risks. When arrested, their usual responses go something like this: "It was so stupid!" "I have never done anything like this in my whole life." "I don't know what got into me."

Of all the sad stories I hear as a priest, some of the saddest are those coming from normally good people who ruin their lives in an instant by doing something that even they will admit was stupid. My heart usually bleeds for them, and compassion rushes over me, because I believe that any of us are capable of about anything in a given circumstance, no matter how much we might deny it. As Friedrich Nietzsche put it, "For every man there exists a bait which he cannot resist swallowing."

How many times have we been severely tempted, but breathed a sigh of relief when we decided to say "no" at the last second, saving us from some awful catastrophe? How many of us have hated ourselves because we lost control of our conscience and decision-making process at the last second (sometimes with the help of alcohol and drugs and sometimes without) and have had to live with painful, permanent consequences? A good life can be spared by a good choice or a good life ruined forever by a bad choice, sometimes in a split second.

What I am talking about here, ultimately, is the idea of "self-control" in the face of temptation, something TV seems to tell us, in so much of its programming, is in short supply. It seems to consistently promote Oscar Wilde's cynical quote, "The only way to get rid of temptation is to yield to it!"

To practice self-control, you have to have it. Self-control takes focused practice and the discipline of an Olympic athlete. "You have to decide what your highest priorities are and have the courage to say *no* to other things. And the way to do that is by having a bigger *yes* burning inside you" (Steven Covey).

To exert power over temptation and "have that bigger *yes* burning inside you," you must be firmly anchored, continuously fed and eternally vigilant. Another way of saying that can be found in one of my favorite Scripture quotes. "He is like a tree planted along the river bank that stretches out its roots into the stream; in the year of drought it shows no distress, but still bears fruit" (Jeremiah 17:8).

Conscience whispers, but temptation leans on the doorbell. Don't answer!

*September 8, 2011*

# Give and "Never Look Back"

*Tell them to do good, to be rich in good works, to be generous, ready to share. I Timothy 6:17*

"Always act on a generous impulse." I read that somewhere and have tried to find out where it came from, but all I could come up with was "anonymous." I think it caught my attention originally because it is a principle I try to cultivate in my own life.

I try, but I am not always successful. I have found that the longer I wait, the more I am likely to talk myself out of being generous. If I wait too long, and think too much, fear of loss gradually replaces the initial impulse to be generous. I have learned, over the years, that when I have a generous impulse, it is best to act quickly and never look back. I have rarely been disappointed. My generosity, more often than not, has come back to me ten-fold.

I have found that the times when I have been disappointed in being generous were the times I was generous for the wrong reasons: wanting to be thanked, wanting to be praised, wanting to feel generous or wanting to be recognized. Francois de La Rochefoucauld put it cynically. "What is called generosity is usually only the vanity of giving; we enjoy the vanity more than the thing given."

Jesus warned us about the "generosity trap" when he said, "When you give alms, do not let your left hand know what your right hand is doing, so that your almsgiving may be secret. And your Father who sees in secret will repay you." (Matthew 6:3-4) I suppose, even at that, one could spoil their own generous impulse by being generous for the reward they will get from God!

Our impulse to be generous can be stingy in the sense that we want that "generous feeling" without any real pain or loss. Mignon McLaughlin said that "We would all like a reputation for generosity, and we'd all like to buy it cheap."

Jesus tells in so many words that "what goes around comes around." True generosity triggers an abundance of generosity. "Give and gifts will be given to you; a good measure, packed together, shaken down, and overflowing, will be poured into your lap. For the measure with which you measure will in return be measured out to you" (Luke 6:38).

The generous impulse is easy when it is returned to those who are generous to us. To that Jesus said, "If you do good to those who do good to you, what credit is that to you?" (Luke 6:33)

Our generosity can sometimes be nothing more than an attempt to bribe God for a favor. "Lord, if you give me what I want, I will make a nice donation to such and such a charity."

The best reason to give in to the impulse to be generous, I believe, is out of a feeling of gratitude for the blessings one has already been given.

*September 15, 2011*